THE CULT OF
SERVICE EXCELLENCE

HOW TO BUILD A
TRULY CUSTOMER-CENTRIC CULTURE

Published by
LID Publishing Ltd.
One Adam Street, London. WC2N 6LE

31 West 34th Street, 8th Floor, Suite 8004,
New York, NY 10001, U.S.

info@lidpublishing.com
www.lidpublishing.com

A member of:

BPR
Business Publishers Roundtable

www.businesspublishersroundtable.com

Printed by CPI Group (UK) Ltd, Croydon CR0 4YY
ISBN: 978-1-910649-54-1

Cover and page design: Caroline Li

THE **CULT** OF
SERVICE EXCELLENCE

HOW TO BUILD A
TRULY CUSTOMER-CENTRIC CULTURE

Oke Eleazu

LONDON   MONTERREY
MADRID   SHANGHAI
MEXICO CITY BOGOTA
NEW YORK   BUENOS AIRES
BARCELONA SAN FRANCISCO

This book is dedicated to my family. My incredible wife Lisa, for being the rock on which everything I have ever achieved has been built. My two amazing kids, Ruby and Harry, for being an inspiration as well as putting up with me locking myself away for long periods whilst writing this book… "Dad, haven't you finished your story yet"? My Mum and Dad for teaching me and, constantly reminding me, that I could do anything I put my mind to. My brothers and sister, Andi, John and Rebecca, for being great siblings! And all my friends for not taking any of this remotely seriously!

Contents

Contents

Foreword

This book couldn't have come at a better time. As the CEO of one of the UK's biggest supermarkets, I'm acutely aware that our customers' needs and expectations are changing constantly. Making sure we get our service right is just as important as it's always been, if not more so.

The principles in this book have helped our business, and I'm confident they can help yours, too.

A source of competitive advantage

Customer service isn't something any business can afford to be complacent about. Getting this right isn't a 'nice to have' – it's a source of competitive advantage.

At Sainsbury's, we serve 25 million customers every week through 160,000 colleagues in 1,200 stores. Ours is one of the biggest online businesses in the UK. And we operate in one of the most competitive industries around.

In our situation, doing the same as you've always done just isn't enough. To stay at the top of our game, our approach to customer service is always evolving.

I first met Oke in early 2011, when he joined Sainsbury's as Customer Service Strategy Director. Although our customer service was already pretty good, he helped us to see how it could be better. To get us there, he set about applying many of the principles in this book.

Consistency is crucial

Making sure we were consistent was a big part of it. Sometimes, wowing your customers can be as simple as being good every single time they interact with you. That's especially true of a big business like ours.

To achieve that consistency, you need to do two things. You need to measure how well you're performing for customers – and set clears plans and targets for improvement. You also need to make sure you're rewarding your people based on these measures.

We did a lot of work with Oke on what we measured, how we measured it, what we developed and changed, how we communicated progress to colleagues and how we rewarded them. This was evolution rather than revolution, but it worked really well for us.

A customer service culture

What's also fundamental is having a culture where the best interests of the customer are 'hardwired' into the DNA of the business.

Having the right culture grows from creating the right environment. This isn't just about having a few nice words on a wall. It's about making sure all those visions, missions and values translate directly into how people behave in our shops.

In this book, Oke makes this seem simple, and in many ways it is. But just because it's simple, it doesn't mean it's easy. Anyone can say you need to be brilliant at the basics, but it's another story to actually deliver that – and deliver consistently.

What's absolutely clear is that to even get close to achieving a customer-centred culture, everyone in the organisation needs to get behind it. It has to mean something to people.

This book is for every business

All kinds of organisations can learn from this book, whether you're a multi-site, multi-million pound chain, a single salon hairdressers or a local newsagent.

Equally, I think the principles are just as relevant to business-to-business organisations as they are to consumer-facing ones. You still need to understand the needs of your clients, to measure how well you're performing for them, and to make sure your business processes and procedures are designed with them in mind.

With its tried and tested ideas, this book reminds us of things that should be obvious, but are easy to forget. I hope you'll get as much from it as I did.

Mike Coupe
Chief Executive, J Sainsbury PLC

Introduction

The Cult of Service Excellence. Wow, that's a bit strong isn't it? Well, maybe it is or maybe it isn't … the purpose of this book is to explain how the environment and culture created in some of the world's greatest customer-focused companies resemble the mind-set created by a cult. In order to do this, we must first understand the characteristics of a cult. Although there are a many definitions, let's try these out for size:

1) A group that loves something … really devoted fans
2) A religion whose beliefs are different than those around it
3) A religious group that is exclusive, secretive, and authoritarian

All of the above sound a bit heavy, and bring to mind the stereotypical images of 'hippy communes' in the '70s, listening to bad music, and wearing even worse clothes! So consider, what are the characteristics of a company that is obsessed with making its customers happy? An organization that continually asks customers what they want and doesn't rest until it is able to meet their needs, consistently … a company that puts the needs of customers ahead of any of its stakeholders, even its shareholders? Organizations like these tend to have incredibly strong, inspirational, and charismatic leaders with a strong singular purpose and great belief. Their passion and vision lead to a devout and dedicated following, employees look up to them and hang on their every word. These organizations also have a very strong sense of what they want to achieve and, more importantly, how they want to achieve it. They have an extremely strong culture and a set of behavioural norms – or even rules – that guide how everyone within the organization should function. They accept like-minded people with open arms, but viciously reject nonbelievers. Basically, they think that "their way is the only way that makes sense."

You wouldn't be hard pushed to fit that description into one of the previous definitions of a cult, perhaps into all three. Therefore, customer-obsessed organizations are a bit like cults. This seems like a simple explanation, if only it was that easy to create a customer centric culture, this would be a very short book … well, much shorter, anyway!

So, where did the idea of truly customer-focused organizations being similar to cults come from? A few years ago, when I was Customer Service Strategy Director at Sainsbury's, I was speaking to a colleague at Sainsbury's Bank. We were talking about the possibility of putting together a best-practice study tour for senior managers and directors, so they could really get an understanding of 'what good looks like' for a customer-centred business. Come to think of it, that study tour still hasn't happened; I must give her a ring!

Anyway, I was reeling off a number of target companies that we could visit, companies that I considered to be extremely good in this 'space' and where I might have a cat's chance in hell of lining up a visit. Initially, I was quite reticent to mention a bank that I had visited recently and was incredibly impressed by: Metro Bank. However, as my list began to dry up after only two or three names, I felt compelled to mention Metro Bank. No sooner had the word 'Metro' crept forth from my lips than a look – a cross between horror, distaste, and bewilderment – came across her face.

It was too late to pretend that I hadn't said it, so I decided to rely on that old and often incorrect saying that "Attack is the best form of defence." I've never much liked that saying; to me defence is the best form of defence, as often showcased by my ability to run away from 'bad' situations and survive! I pronounced that I had spent a reasonable amount of time with the management of Metro Bank (not true) and I thought that they were incredible (perhaps slight exaggeration … to which you will find I am prone). Clearly, the strength of my lucid (and short) argument knocked her back and the rather strange look on her face gave way to one of more contemplative reflection. Now the facts are that Metro Bank is the fastest growing bank in Western Europe, despite being based only in London and the South East of England. They have won numerous awards for their customer experience and their approach is entirely focussed on doing what is right for their customers, so they develop 'focused' not 'customers'.

After a few minutes of silence, she uttered the magical words: "I'm not sure about them, Oke. Aren't they a bit like a cult?" Those words are not in the slightest bit magical, however, in the context of a book entitled *The Cult of Service Excellence*. I think you'll agree it was a pretty seminal moment!

Having said that, there was no 'aha' moment, no flashing light bulbs or bolts of lightening, but it did get me thinking ... like a *cult* ... interesting! This seemed like an odd thing to say, even a bit nasty, if she had little experience with the organization, so I asked her to expand on her statement and what had given her such a negative perception. It transpired that she had actually visited Metro Bank during her time working for Sainsbury's Bank. While she was there, she had seen and experienced a rather worrying ritual, which caused her to draw her rather stinging conclusion. On most Mondays at Metro Bank headquarters in Holborn, induction sessions were presented for all new recruits. Nothing unusual there; we've all done them, normally a moderately dull session led by a slightly boring but somewhat enthusiastic member or two of the Learning and Development team. New employees normally hear all about the mission, vision, and values of the organization, but more importantly, all about health and safety procedures, including fire alarms. And even more importantly, they get their photos taken for their security passes!

Anyway, apparently, this is not the case at Metro Bank. They may also do those boring bits, but at some point in the induction, they lead all the new recruits on a mass conga line around the office, in full view of everyone, and to which they get applause and encouragement. That's right, the conga – normally the preserve of drunken weddings, birthdays, and funerals – with new employees snaking around the room and kicking one leg out to every beat while shouting "ay-ay ay- a-conga" ... yep, that's the one! Can you imagine having to explain that to your kids when you return from the first day at your new high-powered job?

What sort of company would force its new employees to embarrass themselves in this way? What sort of company would have existing employees clapping and encouraging this debacle? What sort of company would brainwash these employees into thinking that this was an acceptable way to behave in the workplace and even convince them that they had enjoyed themselves? My colleague concluded that this could only be the work of an organization that was operating a bit like a cult. I think that this was a pretty reasonable assumption to make. (By the way, you'll find out about the 'the kind of company' Metro Bank is when I cover it later in the book ... I love everything about it ... especially the conga!)

This interesting and amusing tale – which I didn't believe at first, but have since had verified by senior heads at Metro Bank, got me thinking. I had spent some time with the most senior people at Metro Bank, and although I hadn't witnessed the conga, what I had seen was an unswerving and embedded commitment to doing the best for customers and building a deep and loyal relationship with them. I had badgered, probed, and poked to try and find a weakness in their ethos and values, and none was really forthcoming. They were by no means perfect, but their focus was laser-sharp, their commitment indomitable. More than that, every single person I met seemed to get 'it'; they were all singing from the same hymn sheet and wearing the same underpants! It was to some degree unnerving and difficult to describe, so when my colleague described it as a cult, it instantly made sense to me. What's interesting is that cultures of total dedication only look strange from the outside. Not only does everyone inside them tend to agree with each other, they also seem to want to help each other and make the 'right' things happen in line with what they believe.

It made me think of some of the other great organizations in the customer experience-engagement-relationship, space that I have studied, spent time with, researched, or just experienced. Disney, Apple, Amazon, Zappos, Emirates, Virgin, John Lewis, Nordstrom,

South Western, First Direct, QVC all exhibit similar traits, barring the conga, of course. So perhaps this hypothesis has legs. If we can understand the 'anatomy' of these service-excellence cults, then perhaps, just perhaps, we will be able to help lots of other organizations on their customer excellence journeys.

So, if you want to know what makes customer-driven organizations tick and how to build your own customer-driven culture ... please read on!

My intention, when I set out to write this book, was to write a business book that people might want to read ... I know, a very curious concept! Not necessarily all of it, but at least some bits of it – and that in reading some bits of it, they might find those bits entertaining and informative enough to read other bits, without ever having to commit to reading the whole thing ... although that would be lovely.

Additionally, I have tried to avoid all jargon. I can't stand jargon, which I believe was invented only to make people who don't know very much sound clever, or at least cleverer! Now, this is counterintuitive for a business-related book, because I believe the more jargon, frameworks, and charts that are in your book, the smarter you look. So, for that reason, I have stuck in a couple.

And to be frank, research isn't my thing, either. What I mean by research is lots of number crunching and factual verification of what I'm talking about. Instead I have spent time speaking to a lot of people who know what they're talking about; you'll have to trust me on that, too. So what you have are my thoughts based on quite a few years' experience and also their experiences, based on many more years. I'm standing on the shoulders of numerous giants, but rest assured that none of them were injured in the writing of this book ... I'm not that heavy!

Now, I'm sure some of you are wondering why would any organization would want to be like a cult … cults are bad, they brainwash people and control their actions, and bad things tend to happen with them! I get that and tend to agree, but I'm not talking about scary cults! To me, the key reason that organizations looking to build a customer-centric culture need to be like a cult is *belief*! As we will discover, the most customer-focused businesses have a level of commitment to customers that is exceptional. This commitment runs throughout the whole organization, from the CEO to the most junior member, and guides their actions and, even more importantly, every decision that they make. For this to have any chance of happening, everyone has to believe in doing the right thing for the customer. I often describe being customer-focused as a religion; the belief has to be that strong and totally universal. In many ways there are no half measures, you can't 'kind of' believe … ultimately this will not work. If you want to know how these organizations do it and learn how you might do it in your own organization, read on!

CHAPTER ONE

At Disney, Everyone Picks Up Litter!

Indoctrinate means to teach (a person or group) to accept a set of beliefs uncritically.

Here's how it all started...

Most people follow a path they are passionate about, a path discovered after a pivotal moment or event that has caused that interest – or at worst, obsession. Therefore, it's probably worth understanding what caused my obsession with service excellence and how to achieve it.

Without going into the ins and outs of my career (it's in the back of the book), suffice to say that by 2003, I had done rather well. I was working for the Prudential Insurance Company, one of the largest in the UK, with 18 million customers. I'd had some senior roles, been involved in a couple of high profile projects and most importantly, managed a few hundred people who were providing service to customers. To be fair, I was a good operations manager … I knew how to manage the numbers, the importance of having happy people, and that the fewer mistakes we made for customers, the happier they were. This rudimentary set of skills served me well, and in the autumn of 2003 I was lucky enough to be appointed as customer service delivery director. A slightly ambiguous title, it meant that I was suddenly 'in charge' of 3,500 staff across three sites serving millions of customers … pretty cool!

The Pru, as it's called, was a 'mighty business' at the time; so naturally, I felt some pressure to ensure that customers received the service they expected. This was made slightly more difficult because the Pru had a history of 'door-to-door' sales agents … 'The Man from the Pru'. They had been famous and a part of UK culture for 150 years. However, these men and women were more than sales people; they became family friends to their clients. I remember as a kid hurting my leg and needing to go to the hospital. It was our 'Man from the Pru' who happened to be 'visiting' who took me to the hospital in his car. In many ways, this was the ultimate in personalization: these agents knew everyone in the family, they knew the family's important life stages, and they were there every month to reassure you that your money was safe and to answer any questions. Now, I don't want to romanticize them too much, as they got some stuff wrong, too; however, there was a visceral connection between them and their customers that was almost impossible to replace. I know, because a couple years before I was appointed, the Pru had closed their direct salesforce and replaced them with call centres, which were about to be run by me. This replaced the family friend with the faceless efficiency of people our customers had never met.

The call centres had been working well enough, but clearly, it was not the same and customers were feeling the difference. Interestingly, the rate at which policies were surrendered increased, because there wasn't anyone visiting customers to say, "Now, I don't think you want to do that." It's much harder to have that conversation over the phone!

It became clear to me that we had to up our game in terms of service. Even if we had the best customer service in the world, and we didn't, we would struggle to replace the personal touch of 'Man from the Pru'. So how could we be the best for our customers that we possibly could be? It became clear that I needed inspiration from outside the regular financial institutions and perhaps even from outside the UK. Fortunately, one day when flicking through a business magazine, I stumbled across an advert for a study tour to visit Disney University (now the Disney Institute) in Orlando to learn how to create magical customer experiences, from the people who have been doing it since 1955. This caught my eye, although I'm not entirely certain what attracted me the most, the thought of learning from the best, or a week in the sun in Orlando! I was convinced this would spark my enthusiasm and creativity around customer experience and take my thinking to the next level. However, it was not the norm for the organization to send its executives on what might be perceived as a jolly to America, let alone to Disney World in Florida … this was going to be a tough, nigh on impossible sell, but you know what they say, "If you don't ask, you don't get."

So I decided to get the blessing of the boss, then CEO Mark Wood. I thought convincing Mark would be a really tall order because I wasn't sure he would see the benefits of such a trip, and also because he's actually really tall! At that time we were in the middle of a significant transformation of the business and the thought of having to convince him of the benefits of me flying across the Atlantic to visit Mickey Mouse seemed very, well, Mickey Mouse! When the time came for the conversation, I made sure that I had covered the run-of-the-mill update stuff before dropping in the idea of my trip … with a very long pause and a hefty 'gulp'. After surprisingly little thought, he agreed to my request, but put a significant clause on it: I could go, as long as I brought back some skills and ideas that I could share with the rest of the senior management team. This proviso was very important, as it meant that my jolly, sorry, I mean training, was about to be a lot less jolly. I'd actually have to listen to the whole thing and ensure that I had something to share with management! However, in hindsight, the focus that I put into it really shaped my thinking for the next 15 years.

Disney Really Is the Magic Kingdom!

Off I headed to Orlando, for what would turn out to be a life-changing trip. I learned so much on that trip, much of which is laced into different elements of this book. Disney is still one of the most customer-centric places on Earth and there have been many books written about how they achieve this. But there were a couple of stories that showed that a really great customer-centric business would have to think in a completely different way … a way that I very much doubted we at the Pru would be able to do!

First, there were about 150 people on the course and the lectures took place in SeaWorld. Now I've been to many lecture theatres in my time, and most of them you would forget as soon as you left them, but not this one. Imagine all those dull lecture theatres you have sat in, imagine the lecturer or speaker on a stage – and now imagine the backdrop being the giant aquarium at SeaWorld! That's right, if you ever got bored with the presentations, you could always spend your time looking at the stingrays, sharks, and hundreds of other fish. It was an incredible setting for learning.

The first presenter came on stage and asked a very simple question: "Please stand up if you have been to Disneyland before." I remained seated, as it was my first trip, but seeing as this was predominately an American audience, everyone else stood up … which made me want to stand up too, but it was too late, I was already identified as slightly strange! I was very impressed by the fact that so many people had been to Disneyland before, but then the second question came: "Please sit down if you have only been once." To my amazement only about 10% of the audience sat down. Then the next question: "Please sit down if you have only been twice," and another 20% sat down. At this point the majority of the attendees remained standing and had been to Disneyland more than three times, incredible! But there was more to come. I won't go into the sequence of the next questions, as I think you get the drift, but suffice it to say that there were still plenty of the audience standing when he got to 10 times, and when I say plenty, I mean maybe 10% of the group! It was a very simple but effective exercise that delivered a clear message: *Disneyland is a business that is all about repurchase;, if a guest only visits once, they will have considered themselves to have failed.* What that means is that the whole business is geared up around making the experience such that the guests will not only want to tell other people, but more importantly they will want to come back. Imagine a business where everyone is singularly focused on making customers want to come back. This on its own would create an environment in which doing the right thing for customers was the primary focus. But when you think about it, shouldn't this be the case for all businesses?

If you add to that Disney World's theme, which at the time was "We create happiness," you can see that they have a unifying reason for being. We'll come back to this when we cover mission and purpose in later chapters; however, you can see how this culture drives the amazing stories of exceptional service that we hear about Disneyland. One of my favourites was a complimentary letter that they read to us. It was from parents who had just finished their holiday the week before. They had written to say how much they had enjoyed their trip with their two young children and how they couldn't wait to visit again (obviously!). More specifically, they wanted to mention how the cleaners in the hotel had "made their holiday." Not Mickey or Minnie or Dumbo, but the cleaners! Apparently the first day the family returned from an exhausting day at the park, they were ready to go to bed. So they sent the kids to their rooms, only to be surprised by mass hilarity emanating from the kids' bedrooms. With the kids screaming for them to come and have a look, they did just that and saw that the children's teddy bears had been arranged as if they were going on their own adventure! The kids loved this and, as we all know, happy kids equals happy parents! Even more interesting was that every day they came home the bears had been off on a different adventure, to the point that toward the end of the holiday the kids were so keen to see what the bears had been up to that they wanted to leave the park early. Needless to say, they were never let down: the bears were always up to something! What an amazing way to create an emotional connection with customers and almost guarantee their return. Although the magic came from an unlikely source, it was just as important as what was happening in the park. Now, I have no idea if the cleaners are told to create bear adventures, but the point is that they are invested enough in the mission of 'creating happiness' and they are empowered to make the 'magic' happen for the kids. When I hear stories like this, I can't help but think about the power of creating a vision or purpose that people can believe in and sign up to emotionally, providing a greater purpose that would guide their every work moment. Is that indoctrination? Perhaps.

The Magic Is in the Detail

One of the other amazing things about Disney World is the incredible attention to detail. This focus on detail comes from Walt and Roy Disney's near-obsession with making the park perfect for every guest. One of my favourite facts is that they paint the golden railings at the entrance every night! Why? Well it's obvious when you think about it: Disneyland is all about magic and repurchase. If it is your first time, you have probably saved up a lot of money for you and your family to visit the Magic Kingdom, you've probably been waiting for months, and finally the big day arrives. You and the family are walking up to the gates … what you see and experience needs to be everything that you ever imagined for the last few months, maybe even years. Are the railings in front of you gleaming as you imagined? Of course, they need to be! It's no different if you are a returning guest; will the park be just as magical as it was last year? Of course, it needs to be! The only way Disney can achieve that level of emotional connection with customers is to paint the railings every day … there is no other way, no shortcuts. Everyone must buy into 'creating happiness', there are no temptations to just make do and mend. A painted railing means a painted railing. In reality, there is a night crew of around 600 people painting, fixing, cleaning, pruning, and mending things around the park, 365 days of the year. Every one of these people knows that they have a key role in making the magic happen for their customers … they are key cogs in the wheel.

One of the things that not a lot of people know about Disney World in Florida is that it's built on the first floor! Basically, underneath the Magic Kingdom are miles and miles of tunnels that staff, or as they call them, 'cast members', can get around the park without being seen by customers. However, the reality is that they are not tunnels, as they were not excavated out of the ground. They were actually built first and the park was built on top of them ... hence the park being on the first floor! The story of how this came to happen is a testament to Walt Disney's vision and his commitment to improve service for customers. One of the things that really irritated him about Disneyland in Anaheim, California, his first theme park, was that it was possible to see the Disney characters walking around the park to get into the right positions. In fact, legend has it that Walt himself once saw Mickey take his head off in the park. I'm sure that was traumatic for him, but what about the poor kids who were traumatized for the rest of their lives – Mickey really isn't a 5-foot mouse with a squeaky voice, he's a man with a beard! This may seem amusing to you and I, but this would have been deeply troubling for Walt. Disney is all about magic, and the whole point of magic is that you don't know how it happens, you can't know how it happens, and Disneyland in Anaheim was failing on that count. He decided that there had to be a better way, and hence the tunnels of Orlando were born. One man's vision and commitment to excellence, with a whole organization believing in that purpose, means that anything can happen and anything can be built. Very few organizations have that sort of commitment, but that's what it takes to be the best.

As part of the course, I was lucky enough to visit the tunnels to see how the whole 'other' world of Disney World operates. It really is the most amazing thing. You disappear around the most innocuous corner and then down some stairs and you enter this incredible subterranean world, with Disney characters, heads off, whizzing around on golf buggies to get to the right place. There are people discussing plans loudly and others eating and others just hanging out. There are maps and schedules everywhere, and they are seriously needed. If I went down there without a guide, I'm not sure I'd ever get out, and I'd have to live in this slightly whacky alternative world, like something out of an art movie. Anyway, while I was down there I was looking at one of the very complex schedules on the wall, and I was joined by a cast member looking up where he was supposed to be. We started a conversation. By the way, everyone down there was incredibly friendly, a smile and hello for everyone. We were clearly guests, but it didn't seem to matter; everyone seemed to be having a ball and had time to interact. Clearly, I knew they had to be like this in the park, but you always imagine that once the cast members had 'crossed the white line' they would shake off that cheerfulness, rejoice in being miserable, and kick any available cats. But not a bean of it, they were *all* incredibly lovely; in fact, it was eerily cheerful, a bit like a cult (I didn't have the idea at that point, but looking back, it was obvious!). While there might have been some element of cultural indoctrination, the reality is that it's really difficult to make people be happy all the time; the right thing to do is recruit happy people.

I was curious as to how it all worked, how the cast members knew where they needed to be and how the complex plan worked. Obviously, the cast member was more than happy to talk me through it all. However, the more he talked the more I realized how much of it was dependent on individuals taking accountability for their part of the plan and that if they didn't, the whole thing would fall apart! This prompted the obvious question for me: "What happens if someone calls in sick?" I was struggling to see how this would all hold together if one or two people decided that they weren't up to it on any given day! Interestingly, the response was not a long and convoluted diatribe about contingency plans, but simply, "That almost never happens!" Having managed a few thousand people, I found that hard to believe, so I pressed, but received the same response. The explanation was again a very simple, but incredibly powerful and inspirational one. He said, "We all know what our jobs are and why we are here ... to make magic happen for all the customers that come and visit the park, so it takes a lot to stop us from coming in and getting our jobs done!" Yet another 'wow' moment on the visit. There was absolutely nothing cynical or sarcastic about what he was saying; he believed it and so did others I spoke to. They may have expressed it in different ways, but the message was the same: "We are connected to the mission of this business, we believe in it, and we are going to do our best to make it happen, to make the vision a reality."

I was clear on what I had seen and experienced, but I was less clear about how they made it happen: how did they clone these people, how did they make them 'dream the dream', and how did they make them turn up for work every day with smiles on their faces? When I explored this, I found that Disney has very low staff absenteeism and also very low turnover, a kind of devotion to the job and to the company and this became clearer later in the visit. There are hundreds of roles at the Walt Disney World Resort, but there is only one purpose:

"To make sure that every guest has the most fabulous time of his or her life."

Lee Cocerell, EVP Operations, Disney World

At Disney, Everyone Picks Up Litter

Apparently, when Walt Disney first told his wife that he was going to open a theme park, she responded very negatively, stating that all theme parks were grotty and dirty. He responded by saying, "That's the point, mine will never be dirty."

In that one sentence he established a mind-set that is still present today. On our last day of the course, we had another guided tour of the park, but this time we pretty much knew how it worked … the park had given up some of its magic but not all! The tour was to be conducted by one of the most senior vice presidents, and beforehand he came into the auditorium for a final question-and-answer session. The place was packed and numerous questions were asked and beautifully answered, one of which still sticks in my mind. A lady in the audience, who had clearly been to the park on many occasions, pointed out how clean the park always was, no matter what time of the day, so she asked how this was achieved. She knew about the night-shift workers mentioned earlier, but presumed that there must be a daytime equivalent, which I was sure that there was. However, that was not the answer she was given. Calmly, the very senior guy at the podium uttered one of my favourite quotes ever: "At Disney, we all pick up litter, and when I say all, I mean all, from the most senior to the most junior. It's all of our jobs to keep the park clean." This may seem like nothing, but it meant everything to me. Not only did they have great people working for them who were linked strongly to an inspirational purpose, but they had leaders who were willing to lead by example in establishing what needed to happen, no matter how menial the task! I had never really made these links before, but as I listened to what he had to say, it all made perfect sense. It was like an epiphany – this was my Road to Damascus, just with big mouse ears!

This was great. I kind of got it and set off on the tour a very happy man. Wandering around in the Florida sunshine felt great, watching all of the happy customers living the dream, all the happy cast members making the dream come true, and chatting to colleagues about how amazing it all was. Then it happened, so subtly and unheralded that you could have missed it. The very senior guy showing us around spotted an ice cream wrapper on the ground, and he gently swooped and picked it up, spun around, and put it in the bin, all without missing a step. It was as if the clouds parted and a choir sang 'Halleluiah'! He was a leader that actually walked the talk and did exactly as he expected from his colleagues – no wonder it all worked! You may be thinking that he did that for effect and I would think the same; however, what he did was instinctive, not thought through, and the reality is that I saw him do it on several occasions during our walk around; it was just something that he did.

What this told me was that the leaders in this organization walked the talk and in doing so empowered everyone else to do likewise.

All in all, you can see why this was such a valuable and life-changing trip. I learned a lot from that tour and successfully took these ideas back to base camp, and they became key in developing our customer experience strategy. In addition, my experience left me with beliefs that I have taken forward, and much of this I will refer to throughout this book. In reality, when I got back from my trip, everyone assumed I'd been on a jolly and teased me endlessly about it! However, in the mix of all the amazing things I saw and learned, a few things stood out:

- Create a vision, purpose, or product that people can and will believe in.
- Hire people who will buy into this vision and accept it as their own and look for opportunities to make a difference.
- Hire and develop leaders who will walk the talk, lead from the front, and create an environment for everyone to achieve the overall mission of the organization.

Sounds easy, right? It's one of those easy-to-say, difficult-to-do situations. However, we are starting to see similarities between what we talked about with Metro Bank and Disney and general cult-like behaviours. Let's revisit the Disney scenario and check: clear vision of what the organization wants to achieve for its customers, visionary and uncompromising leaders, staff who buy into the vision and direction and are devoted to the achievement of its goals, as well as rejection of those that don't fit; middle leadership that ensures the right environment is in place and encourages compliance; followers who buy into the vision and understand not only their role in achieving it but also how they need to behave to make it happen; and last but not least, total devotion to its customers. I think its a check-off for all. Now we are beginning to build a compelling argument for this cult thing. Let's see where this goes!

CHAPTER TWO

Why Customer Service Really Does Matter!

Why now?

So Disney is good at it, and Metro Bank is good at it … so what? Most organizations have customers of some sort and many have been very successful for years without showing any cult-like characteristics. Why has it suddenly become more important and almost a buzzword in every organization's strategy?

The first thing to note is that numerous organizations have been saying that customers are important for many years. In fact, they've been saying this forever, but in reality it just wasn't true. I always say that if you were to line up the CEOs from the top 100 companies and ask them if their customers and the service and experiences they provide to their customers were of prime importance, it's likely that 95% of them would agree strongly. If that was the case, then why for so many years have customers been treated poorly? Although 'the customer is king' is a truism, in reality customers have had very little power and they certainly weren't king, queen, or any other member of the royal family for that matter. Most organizations said that customers were at the heart of their businesses, but they were really just a part of the commercial mix … probably more important than employees, but much less important than shareholders.

Most customer service directors, myself included, would find it incredibly difficult to secure investment into a customer-service function unless something was terminally broken or there was some sort of 'burning platform'. This is because customer service was – and still is – seen as a cost centre, a cost of doing business and not as a revenue-generating profit centre. This may sound a bit like business mumbo-jumbo, but it's incredibly important in understanding how decision-making has been made around customer service. Every business wants to be more efficient and to reduce costs to improve margins and become more competitive. The problem comes when you run a big cost centre like customer service, the organization is always looking for you to 'squeeze the pips' and cut costs. Most companies want to keep the level of service the same with less money. I was lucky enough to work in enlightened companies, where ***the request was often to create better service with less money ... more for less!*** If customer service is seen as a cost centre, then any cost cutting will, normally, be felt by the customer ... but that doesn't matter, does it?

"Oh No, I've Got to Ring the Call Centre"!

There is no field where this focus on costs is more evident than contact centres or call centres. If you are anything like me, you'll be filled with dread at the thought of having to call a big organization! The best way to understand this is to relate a recent experience I had, one that is by no means uncommon. Once I have related this story, we'll go back and unpack it to see how it has its roots in un-customer-centric decisions probably driven by cost pressures.

Last week I had to ring a very large telecom provider about some issues on my account. My problems seemed reasonably complex, so I decided to ring, rather than to use any of the other channels of communication that were open to me. The first challenge was actually finding a telephone number to ring! It wasn't on any of the documentation, and it was not obvious on the website. When I finally found a 'contact us' part of the website, I had to try and work out what type of customer I was before I could even decide which number to use. I finally decided on the most suitable number and dialled through, only to be greeted by the familiar Interactive Voice Response (IVR) machine! We went through the normal song and dance, my name and what I was calling for, which is always my favourite bit because what you are calling for rarely fits into any of the categories given, so you end up guessing and hoping for the best, although I always try to wait for the last option: 'none of these'. If you're really lucky, you might get to play the password game! It's always impossible to remember your password without writing it down, but everyone tells you that you shouldn't write your password down. So you finally finish the IVR lottery and the system helpfully tells you that your query can probably be answered 'if you visit our website'.

Some systems, infuriatingly, cut you off at this point; however, this one didn't. It asked me to hold for one of its operatives. Normally you would be excited that you had almost made it to a real human being, but I was ever cautious; I had done this too many times before and I knew there was still a long way to go. And then you hear it, the words that you have been secretly dreading: "Due to extremely high call volumes at present, unfortunately all our operatives are busy, please hold and an operative will be with you as soon as they can." That's right, you have entered the first 'black hole of hold doom'! I had to make a decision: do I put the phone down immediately, not invest any more of my precious time and go through this purgatory later or, do I hold and face an infinite wait? I decided to hold, a decision that was immediately rewarded with that terrible on-hold music, which was followed by the annoying, most nonsensical statement ever created a minute later: "Your call is valuable to us, so please continue to hold." This statement is repeated every 90 seconds, and each time is like another dagger through your heart. Ideally, when on hold, the speaker function is particularly helpful so that you can do something else and make the most of your time. However, in this case this didn't work; the infuriating music was infuriatingly low and I could barely hear it. Every 90 seconds it stopped and there was silence, a silence that filled me with hope that someone might actually pick up my call, but then either the music started again or the crazy message. What this meant, was that I couldn't get on with anything else. I was just in an endless loop of raised and dashed expectations. If you think about it, it's almost like some form of torture – in fact, it feels like it is!

Eventually, after 25 minutes of having my fingernails pulled out, someone finally answered the call. I should have been angry, possibly fuming that I'd wasted half an hour of my life on this and that I'd never get that time back, but I was actually grateful to be finally talking to a human being! The positive feeling was short lived when the guy on the end of the line proceeded to ask me all the same questions as the computer did half an hour ago. *Why*? This included the dreaded password question, which I apparently got wrong ... why didn't the bloody computer tell me that? It could be your mother's maiden name, it could be a memorable place, it could be the name of your first kitten! The additional issue was that, due to the delay on the line, he was clearly in India somewhere. Now, I must say at this point that I love India, and I have been responsible for a number of call centres out there, but it does slow things down because I have to spell everything out using the phonetic alphabet ... 'e' for Echo, 'c' for Charlie, and so on. We got there eventually, and after he had dispensed the normal pleasantries, I explained the issue to him. Thankfully, he said that he understood, but (and you know what's coming here) I've come through to the wrong department. *Aarrgghhh*, can this really be happening? Well yes, it happens all the time! Sensing my frustration, he told me not to worry, that he could get me through to the right department very quickly, and "would I like to hold?", to which I replied that, no I would not. He replied that he couldn't transfer me if I didn't. So why did he ask in the first place? After three minutes of being on hold with no music, which I decided was worse than the music, I was in the capable hands of someone who could sort out my query, which she did quickly and efficiently. At the end she says politely, "Is there anything else we can help you with today?" *Help me*? No chance – there's no way I'm going to risk that level of torture again today; but yes, I would like to complete the survey.

Why Is It Always Like This?

I know it was reasonably tortuous to listen to that story, because it is an all-too-common occurrence for almost everyone, in many cases even worse. Surely the simplest thing for an organization to do is to handle a query; how can such a painful process make customers feel that the organization likes them, cares about them, or even respects them – all the things that would create a sense of customer loyalty to that business? This all goes back to my earlier point that call centres are normally relatively big, labour-intensive functions, and when the cost-pressure man comes for his 10% savings, the call centre is where he's going to come knocking first. In reality, call-centre technology enables companies to predict call volumes and ensure that they have enough people to take the calls when they hit. Obviously it's not that simple, but that's the gist of it. However, call-centre staff cost money, so if the organization runs short of a few people, all that happens is that the wait times get longer, and that's okay, isn't it? Although there are plenty of exceptions, it's fairly safe to assume that if your call isn't being answered, there aren't enough people to answer the calls – which saves them money!

But what about the other issues that were raised by my call, are they all about costs? Firstly, I struggled to find the number; trying to find the call-centre number on a website is fast turning into an Olympic sport! There is a very simple reason for that: they don't want you to call. Self-service is one of the biggest trends in customer management, and on the surface it seems good for customers. Customers can look for the answers to their queries on the websites' Frequently Asked Questions (FAQs) page or customer communities pages; they can do it in their own time and often get answers from people who have experienced the same problem. The benefit for the organization is that a large number of customers no longer ring the call centre and so they require less people on the phones and therefore save money. And as the 'bank' of answers grows, less calls are received and more money is saved.

The problem is that it doesn't always work like that! I have implemented this sort of system a couple of times and what tends to happen is that you start to get thousands and thousands of 'hits' on your FAQs, but very little reduction in phone calls – almost as if customers find an answer and then want to confirm it! The problem for organizations is that they are now paying for a new FAQ system as well as all the people handling the calls, i.e., it's more expensive, not cheaper, therefore something's got to give. The system's already been paid for, so the only solution is to reduce call volumes and the way many organizations do that is by 'hiding' the telephone number. That's not very customer driven, but it is very cost driven!

Are the dreaded IVRs used to save money? On the surface, IVRs were created to make life easier for customers by ensuring that their calls were routed to a department and person that could help. However, in reality, they also allow organizations to route calls through to agents with limited skill sets, which makes training and dealing with attrition easier. And guess what, fewer people are needed! The other issue is that if you end up in the wrong place, that person can't help you and has to find someone else who can. And to cap it all, customers hate them, as they have been overly designed with multiple layers of hell that don't help at all. In general, I believe that IVRs are a good idea in principle. However, they have been largely abused and have become the least customer-centric device ever invented. But do they save money? Of course they do!

Lastly, let's deal with the delicate issue of outsourcing and off shoring. I say it's delicate, but in many ways it's the simplest of all. Both outsourcing and off shoring are clearly a cost play by organizations, especially when it comes to call centres. Through outsourcing and off shoring, the organization is able to save a 'shed load' of money while at the same time hoping the service will not deteriorate too much. Anyone that says otherwise is lying. Off shoring is a classic case of cutting costs 'in the face of customers' – where they will really notice it. It's a term that I will keep returning to and a real 'schoolboy' error for companies! Customers will always respond badly when it is clear that they are the victims of cost cutting, as was clearly the case with the off shoring of call centres. This enabled organizations that hadn't (yet!) outsourced to gain a competitive advantage and ultimately hastened the return of many call centres back onshore. I genuinely do not believe that off shoring a call centre is a customer-centric thing to do, for a number of technical reasons, but most significantly because customers tend not to like it … and that's good enough for me!

Before I got carried away explaining the terrible and clearly traumatic phone call I experienced, I said that the problem with customer service functions was that they were seen as cost centres; therefore they had to be lean, efficient, and cost effective. The reality is that there are many companies for whom my experience *does not matter* and very few people would know that I was having that experience anyway. Hopefully, my example and the reasoning behind it highlight the implications if a company was to operate like this. I hope it also serves to indicate the massive opportunities that exist if organizations were to change their thinking around customer contact being a 'cost' and think of it as a way of building lasting relationships with customers.

Who wouldn't love a company that made it easy to contact them however you pleased? You could sort out problems for yourself on the website, but if that didn't work out, their number was clearly displayed on the website with the invitation to "Feel free to call us whenever you like!" When you dial through, a human very quickly answered without having to go through an IVR, or if you did, it took your details easily and they were already with the agent and you didn't have to give all of your details all over again. The agent you got to talk to was friendly and extremely knowledgeable about what you wanted and other topics, too. They were able to quickly deal with your initial query and also a supplementary question that you had on a completely different product. At the end of the

39

call, they ask you to fill in a survey, which you gladly do. Moreover, every time you call, you always receive that level of service. Does that feel like a cost centre to you? Sounds like a dream to me. Luckily, these call centres do exist, but only in organizations who take a 'cultish' view of serving customers. Only in organizations where making the customer's life easier is more important than how much money it costs to do so – because a happy customer will buy more and get other people to buy more. To me that makes them a profit centre.

It's All about Power and Control

I've been thinking for a while that the whole thing with customers and organizations is almost like a titanic battle of good versus evil – huge unscrupulous conglomerates with all their money and slick-suited staff against poor individuals who just want what's right – all coming to a cinema near you soon! Actually, there are many films like that, films like *Erin Brockovich*, where the lone individual stood up to the tyranny of the large corporation. To a lesser extent, things do play out like that in reality and that is because it's about power and control. Organizations have traditionally wanted to be in control of their customers: target them, acquire them, and then manage them in the way that they see fit. This may appear like a Dickensian view of the world, but if you stop and think about it for a second, hopefully you will see that it has some merit. I have worked most of my career in financial services, an industry where we would commonly take money from customers, legitimately, like investments, and then make it extremely difficult for them to get the money back – even though it was their money. And to add to that, if they wanted their money back sooner than we had expected, we would adjust the value downward for the inconvenience that they had caused us: how dare they want their own money back? This wasn't exactly very customer-centric, but it didn't matter because the organizations are in control and they can do pretty much whatever they like.

It was that exact disparity in power that led, in part, to a number of financial scandals in the UK over the last 20 years, whether it be the pension miss-selling, where people were convinced to leave perfectly good company pension schemes to buy inferior personal pensions; endowment miss-selling, where people sold endowment policies that would not pay off their mortgages; or payment protection insurance, where people were sold insurance that they just didn't need. Having been involved, to some extent, in clearing up all of these scandals, I have heard many people within the organizations cry foul; what happened to "Let the buyer beware," one of the first rules of contract law? But that's just it: it's not really a fair fight. One part has all the information, the other has virtually none. It's basically David versus Goliath, and David doesn't even have his slingshot! It's also this level of imbalance that has brought about the unprecedented level of consumer regulation ... the march of the regulators. This regulation explosion is a stark admission that we cannot trust our large organizations to treat their customers, the people who pay them money, in an appropriate manner or, as they say, fairly.

So how, in a fair and just society, have we ended up in such a situation, not just in financial services but across all industries, where the picture is the same? I think that's probably the subject for another book, and there are probably plenty of commentators that can do it better justice than me, but from my perspective, due to the huge imbalance of power and control, aligned with the desire to make more and more money, organizations lost respect for their customers and stopped caring about them. Customers became numbers on a spreadsheet and not individuals with lives, families, aspirations, dreams, and disappointments. I was born and bred in South London, and we have an expression: "Are you dissing me?" with the option to add the term 'Bruv'! Dissing is shorthand for disrespecting (if such a verb exists, but I'm sure you get what I mean!). I think this comes from the basic principle that everybody deserves to be treated with respect; it's a basic right.

From a customer-service perspective, I think that organizations have been 'dissing' their customers for years: making me hang on the phone for 45 minutes, sending me the wrong items, making it hard to return the items, not giving me my money back when I can't attend the concert, making me queue in the supermarket for 20 minutes due to a staff shortage, cancelling my flight without telling me. I could go on and I'm sure you could as well. These are all forms of disrespect toward customers. And do the organizations doing these things care? In many cases, they don't.

What's worse is that the less opportunity customers have to exercise their right of choice, the worse the situation becomes. Through my work with the Institute of Customer Service, I have analysed how different industries provide services for their customers. We'll expand on this in later chapters, but there is unequivocal evidence that where the customer has more choice and control – i.e., the ability to take their business elsewhere, quickly and easily – the level of service experienced is significantly better. The best examples of this are retailers. Where it is more difficult to change suppliers, the service is much worse. Utility companies are a good example … it's not easy to move house! This doesn't necessarily mean that retailers endemically care more about their customers than utilities companies, but the balance of power between them and their customers is more even and therefore the commercial implications force them to think differently. And that is why competition and more specifically the ability to 'switch' companies is the biggest cure to this ill. *It gives customers back power and control and allows them to exercise their most powerful weapon: the money in their wallets.*

We've seen this happen to a certain degree in banking in the UK. Banking used to be right up there with utilities (or should I say down there) as being known to provide terrible service to their customers, who effectively saw themselves as hostages. A friend and former colleague, Mike Hobday, now a Partner at IBM, wrote an interesting white paper about how, by their very nature, banks would find it very difficult to be customer-centric because they make a lot of money from things that are bad for customers, such as rolling over debt on credit cards and hefty overdraft charges. This reminded me of a conversation I had with a very senior individual from one of the big credit card companies. She described her 'bad' customers as the ones who paid off their balances on time every month, and her 'good' customers as those who only paid off the minimum every month. I found this totally counterintuitive, but of course she was right: commercially, the customers with the poor financial behaviours made the bank money! And we wonder how we ended up with sub-prime mortgages! However, as the government has leaned on the banks to make switching easier, we have seen an uptick in focus on service with the new entrants into the market. These so-called challenger banks are taking a more customer-driven approach to banking and customers are beginning to switch to them. As a 'rising tide lifts all boats', the sector as a whole has been one of the most improved in the last few years in terms of service, and even the more traditional behemoth banks are being forced to take a more customer-focused approach.

Luckily, the Tide Is Turning

This brings us to one of the most fundamental points in the book: the world is changing and it's changing fast! This has significant implications for customers, businesses, and the balance of power between them. One of the implications of this fast-changing world is the commoditization of goods and services. Because of how quickly research-and-development teams work, and mass production of products in places like China, the reality is that one product is very much like another and long-term differentiation dependent on product features is becoming a thing of the past. A TV is just a TV, a fridge is just a fridge, and a cup of coffee is just a cup of coffee. To be more specific, products in these categories probably do have differences in product features, but the perception by the customer is that they do not; they are just a commodity, like beans and rice – there is no added value in the product. Very few have been able to escape the environment of growing commoditization based on product differentiation only.

So, what are the implications of the growing wave of commoditization? It's got to be good news for customers because it allows them more choice, and choice is good as it shifts the balance of power between customers and organizations back toward customers. If you want to buy a TV, for example, the choice is vast and since one is pretty much like another, companies have to think about how they will convince you, the consumer, to buy their TV. For organizations, this is a more significant problem. Traditionally there are two forms of competitive advantage: cost-price and differentiation. Competing on cost-price is difficult, often leads to reduced margins and profit, and is a slow race to the bottom. A much easier route – and some might say more sustainable – for organizations to differentiate themselves from the rest of the market is around the brand and customer experience. Let's consider for a second the impact of commoditization on a brand.

Let's think about something that is truly commoditized for me: coffee shops! The reason they are a commodity for me is that I don't drink coffee, so tea from one place is pretty much like tea from another. The product features are broadly the same, as is the price, so in what way can the brand influence my decision-making? I'm not a brand expert, but it would appear clear to me that the brand has to offer me something tangible. It either has to say something about me and the kind of person I am and, as we'll see later, even that is becoming less relevant. Or it has to represent a different experience; this is one of the only forms of true differentiation left. So the brand, the product, and the experience become even more inextricably linked, ideally with the customer experience becoming more than an equal partner ... bingo! Organizations have to start thinking about how can they make the customer experience better than that of their competitors. At last, a commercial imperative to improve things for customers, this is a far cry from the hostages that we described earlier. So perhaps there may be a little less 'dissing' in the future. Of course, this only works really well where there is choice. Where there is less choice, real or perceived, the old problems will persist ... or will they? Fortunately, there are other forces at play, the most important being that customers are changing like never before and changing the game forever.

CHAPTER THREE

The Perfect Storm

We are currently experiencing the 'perfect storm' of changing customer behaviours. These changes are fuelled by a number of different factors, but they are very disconcerting for most organizations, as the result is more power and control in the hands of customers – and we know how much businesses don't like that! We'll look at a few of the key factors and start with the most significant in terms of customer behaviour: technology

1. Technology

Technology has been changing all our lives for quite some time. Computerization has created a change in what we can do, how we live, and how we work. However, computerization was only the start of the journey. It's the development of the internet that has caused the biggest cultural change since the industrial revolution in the 18th and 19th centuries. The ability to find information at the click of a button and create communities and share things has changed the way we live forever. More importantly, it has empowered customers like never before, and therefore completely changed consumer behaviour. There used to be a saying that an unhappy customer tells 10 other people; now, due to social media, that number has increased by a magnitude of at least 10. Unhappy customers potentially have a global audience with which to share their grievances or alternatively share their praise. And due to the connected nature of the world, this often snowballs and sometimes goes viral. It's interesting that when you use, for example, Facebook to moan about a particular organization, you can always guarantee that someone else has had the same or similar problem and they are more than happy to share it too. Before you know it, a conversation has started, with others joining in, and with every conversation like this an organization's reputation could be tarnished. Make no mistake: with the invention of the internet and social media, customers now have a voice, both individually and collectively.

My favourite example of an individual making a big enough noise to silence a giant corporation is a story about a gentleman named Dave Carroll, and has come to be commonly known as "United breaks guitars." I will paraphrase the story, but if you want to know the full gory details, guess what – you can Google them! Dave Carroll is a musician, and in 2009 he was flying from Halifax to Omaha, via Chicago, with United Airlines. During his trip his guitar was severely damaged, due to rough treatment by baggage handlers. Mr Carroll contacted United to ask what they would do about it and received some pretty poor responses by all accounts. However, rather than moan about it to friends or even post it so that hundreds of people could see it, he decided to do something quite novel. He decided to write a song called "United Breaks Guitars" and record the song and upload it to YouTube. The video received 150,000 views within one day, five million within a month, and just to prove that social media is a gift that keeps on giving, to date it has been viewed more than 15 million times. Having originally rejected Mr Carroll's claims for compensation, United started running around doing all the normal things that big corporations do to try to avoid a public relations disaster, including asking for permission to use the video as part of their training! However, the die was cast and United's reputation had been severely damaged by one man and his guitar. There have been claims that this actually affected United's stock price and forced them to cancel a national advertising campaign. I'm not sure how true those claims are, but the fact is the internet and social media specifically give customers a voice like never before and start to redress the balance of power. It's not just the customers' ability to take their money elsewhere, it's their ability to shout about poor behaviour and injustice and make others think about taking their money elsewhere too. There is no longer anywhere to hide!

Social Media Fuels Customer Power

The other impact of social media on customer power is that it has given customers another channel with which to interact with organizations, especially when making a complaint. Up until now, all the existing channels – snail mail, email, text, fax, and phone – created a one-to-one relationship between the individual and the organization. This meant that not only was the organization in control of the decisions, it was also in total control of the message and only one person could receive it. This was great: treat customers as poorly as you liked and only they would know ... and the 10 friends they would tell!

However, now it's all changed. In their rush to clamber on the social media bandwagon and interact with customers more, and maybe even sell them some more stuff, most organizations created Facebook pages and Twitter accounts, a marketing person's dream in terms of pushing out messages. However, inadvertently they had opened Pandora's box of complaints! Now, instead of contacting an organization on a one-to-one basis, customers could post their complaints on the organization's Facebook page for everyone to see. Good-bye one-to-one interaction, hello one-to-many! The implications of this are significant. First, it invites the organization to show how it deals with complaints in general, and the specific issue in particular, in full view of many of its other customers. Second, it prompts others who have the same issue to raise it. Third, it sets new expectations for the timeliness with which issues will be resolved. I remember when next-day delivery or service was considered quick – not any more. It also allows people who have a common issue to link together and form a community. I worked with one client for whom there were more 'friends' on the organization's 'I hate xxx' Facebook page, which was created by their customers, than was on its official Facebook page! Most organizations invite customers to post their issues on social media, but prefer to resolve the issues through more traditional, one-to-one channels. Of course, by then the damage is already done and they're rushing to resolve an issue that they might not have done normally ... a great queue-jumping tool!

Also, when are some customers more equal than others? I remember an incident a couple of years ago when I was responsible for the service centres at Sainsbury's. One of my managers called about giving a response to a fairly standard issue that we dealt with hundreds of times a year. In fact, I was surprised to receive the call at all, until I was told that the query had been raised on Twitter by a very famous celebrity, who had five million followers! Worse still, we knew that the standard response that we have given to hundreds of people previously would be unacceptable to the customer! We had two options: give him what he wanted and break with precedent in public, or stick to our guns and take any flak that would come. What would you do? We took the second option on the basis that our reasoning was robust and to change our decision would be unfair and more importantly, visible. It did lead to a bit of an issue, but it was manageable. However, this puts significant pressure on an organization's decision making, both in terms of making the right actual decision and whether to treat people differently because they have a huge following or allowing them to queue jump because they have raised the issue on social media. Different organizations do things differently and I'm not sure that there is a right answer; you really have to judge each individual case on its merits. There is no doubt, though, that social media is the biggest game changer in the power shift between organizations and their customers.

Another incident that happened while I was at Sainsbury's highlights how social media has empowered people to take on and influence even the largest organizations. Throughout the back end of the noughties, extensive coverage was given to the issue of mobile phone hacking by newspapers. This had included public enquiries, House of Commons Select committees, and although it was a high profile story, it really hadn't captured the imagination of the public because this was a story predominantly about rich and famous people having their phones hacked by the papers … terrible, of course, but they are in the public eye! However, everything changed on 4 July 2011 when the *Guardian* published an article claiming that the voicemail of the abducted schoolgirl, Milly Dowling, had been hacked by the *News of the World* back in 2002. This changed public perception around phone hacking and started a movement fuelled by social media to bring the *News of the World* to account. On 7 July, I was in a meeting of the customer-and-colleague team at Sainsbury's, which included the director of corporate affairs. During the morning we started to receive news that hundreds, maybe thousands, of customers were posting to our social media pages that we should stop selling the *News of the World*. The response to that is always a customer-driven one, in that we would continue to sell the *News of the World*, and if customers refused to buy it, then we would rethink our position, i.e., we would allow customers the choice. However, on receiving that response, the threat from the public via social media channels changed to, "If you don't stop selling the *News of the World*, we will never set foot in your shops again."

Whether this would have happened or not, we will never know. However, the sheer numbers and the strength of opinion meant that eventually there was no option but to tell News International, the owners of *News of the World*, that we would no longer be able to sell the paper, a huge decision with huge implications, but created by the collective will of our customers. At the same time, this campaign had been targeting a number of other major retailers that made the same decision, and later that day we heard the incredible news that the *News of the World* was to close at the end of the week! Quite unbelievably, this all happened in *one day*. I'm sure there were many reasons that News International made the decision to close the paper, but I'm sure the weight of public opinion focused through the 'lens' of the powerful retailers was a significant contributing factor. When I reflected on what had happened, I was in awe. To witness the power of the collective customer voice, so close up, was phenomenal. Could this have happened even 10 years ago? I don't think so. Right there and then, I realized that the world of dealing with customers would never be the same again, and social media was the catalyst.

Knowledge Is Power and Customers Have It

In a more practical sense, the internet also gives customers power in another dimension. It gives them access to knowledge, and we all know that knowledge is power. In its simplest terms, knowledge allows customers to better understand how things work and how to compare them. It also allows people to question what they've been told, even by supposed experts. I remember when I was at Bupa talking to a couple of doctors. They told me that nowadays patients often know more about the ailments and drugs they should be taking than the doctors! There is always the issue of a little knowledge being a dangerous thing, but that applies to the doctors and the patients. Basically, the internet has created transparency, something that did not exist before, and transparency changes everything in terms of the transactions and communications between a customer and an organization.

When I was studying economics as a business student, my professors would always talk about a perfect market being one where buyers and sellers in the system had complete information about a product, and it was easy to compare prices (or something like that). I always thought that was impossible, but it was useful in building theoretical situations. However, a few years later, it's not ridiculous at all, and we have situations where the new 'transparent' world allows something close to the 'perfect market'. What we now have are commonly known as aggregators. These are websites or computer programmes that collate information from various sources online to allow comparison of features – and most importantly, prices. Websites like Compare the Market, Money Supermarket, and Kelkoo allow customers to shop around from one website. Their use is growing and in turn it impacts organizational behaviour. Most importantly, it drives further commoditization, as mentioned earlier. When I buy my annual car insurance, I go to money supermarket, which brings up a plethora of options – and I look at price first, features next, and then possibly who's selling it. I related this to an insurance client once, and he was shocked and disturbed that I bought insurance like this, while at the same time extolling the virtues of his product. But most of the things that he was telling me I didn't care about. He and his business had failed to grasp that, in a transparent world, price becomes king and *differentiation becomes harder and harder ... be cheap or be really good at something else that matters to customers.* Most significantly, customers hold all the cards. Funnily enough, the aggregators now have to differentiate themselves from each other. Our favourite offers a free cuddly toy when you shop with them ... we have several in the house now and the kids love them!

The Future Is Mobile

As powerful and revolutionary as both computerization and the web have been, a 'new kid on the block' has driven usage of the internet to a new level over the last few years, and that is mobile devices and smartphones. Devices that allow a customer to access the internet whenever and wherever they want have created the 'always on' generation. There are so many amazing facts about the adoption and penetration of smartphones – I'll let you read them elsewhere, just Google them. However, my favourite is that there are around two billion people worldwide with smartphones – a third of the global population – but using them to call other people is only the fifth most common usage! For customers, mobile amplifies everything that we have been talking about, whether it's to send a complaint email, post it on social media, or even find out the price of a particular item. It's all possible – wherever you are and whenever you want, signal and Wi-Fi permitting! Again, this stacks the cards in favour of the customer and changes the level of expectation.

One of the best examples of this is a concept called 'showrooming'... not rude, I promise! Imagine you are shopping for a new washing machine (I always choose washing machines, not sure why). You stand in front of the myriad possibilities, opening and shutting doors and compartments and maybe even taking advice from an assistant. Once you have decided on the one you want, what's the first thing you do? That's right, take out your smartphone, look up the make and model, and see if you can get it cheaper elsewhere. That's called showrooming and has been the scourge of bricks-and-mortar retailers for the last few years. It's perfect market-meets-mobile technology, and it is clearly a brilliant tactic for customers. What's even better for customers is how retailers need to react to deal with it. Originally, the answer was to ensure there were bad phone reception and no Wi-Fi in the store! But then came the sensible reaction, which was to match the price on the internet … great for customers, but not sustainable for stores due to the fixed costs they have to carry. But the real answer – and the best way for retailers to deal with this – is not by matching prices, but by creating *value*. This is something that I will go on and on and on about in this book! Put simply, what I mean by value is ***understanding what a customer values in an experience over and above its price and giving it to them.***

Value is at the core of differentiation. In this example, adding value might be the physical environment of a lovely showroom; the friendliness, expertise, and availability of an assistant; the availability of the product; different delivery options; offers on complimentary products; or access to face-to-face aftercare. All these things add value to the commoditized product and could make a difference in a sale. Even better, though, is that they are all good for customers and highlight that a brand must work hard to make a difference in the evolving purchase habits of consumers.

The impact of mobile and the always-on environment has also influenced customers' perceptions of timeliness. The ability to contact organizations in the moment, wherever you are, means that waiting for days for a response is a thing of the past. There are now numerous stories of people posting or tweeting about situations that they are in right then and are expecting a solution. KLM, the Dutch airline, has become expert at running around Schipol Airport trying to resolve issues for customers, in the moment, in response to social media comments they have received. A few months ago I found myself tweeting back and forth with another airline about the ability to get on a flight. Unfortunately, it didn't have a happy ending, so I made my displeasure clear for all my followers ... that actually sounds quite grand, but trust me, they're a small but loyal bunch. The point I'm making is that mobility means immediate resolution.

The travel and hospitality industry has also been irrevocably influenced by the growth of mobile and other factors from the digital age, such as user reviews. Previously it had been easy for marketers to control the message of how lovely a resort, hotel, or destination was; customers would have read it and hoped for the best. Again, the tables have been completely turned with the advent of user reviews on numerous websites, and most importantly, the ubiquitous Trip Advisor. Who doesn't read about a hotel or a restaurant and immediately go to Trip Advisor to check out what people who have actually been there think? That's millions of people taking advice from people they will never meet. It brings into sharp focus the element of trust – and the reality that customers still trust each other to be open, honest, and transparent more than they trust organizations. This makes it tough to be a restaurateur or a hotelier, but the reality is that they are being held to account by the people who hand over their money – their customers – and that, generally, has to be a good thing, right? More customer power ... hooray.

Customers Are Becoming More 'Appy'

We can't continue without mentioning the newest kid on the block: the not-so-humble app. In fact, apps have been around as long as computers. But in the mobile revolution, smartphones and tablets have supercharged them.

Apps by their very nature are incredibly customer-focused; they were originally designed to make it easier for customers to access a company's products and services. However, it was the creation of Apple's App Store to support its iPhone that really moved the dial on app development, as standalone apps were created and entire businesses on the back of them. The business model for apps and the web-based businesses that support them are again, by definition, customer-centric. Many apps are free to download or offered at a very nominal price; therefore, the key to their success is volume. If you and I decided to create an app that would be downloaded millions of times, a good starting place would be to think of a customer problem that our app could fix. If we found the right customer problem, that would create demand and demand leads to downloads and downloads mean money! Today, we have the biggest and best brains around the world creating apps and games. That means *there is an app for nearly everything*. The other way that apps raise the bar is that because they are designed to be easy to use, and for a particular purpose, they tend to work. They easily do what they are supposed to, which is why apps have revolutionized gaming, dating, to-do lists, travel, accommodations, fitness, newspapers, communication, listening to music ... the list goes on! All of this happens by striving to make customers' lives better!

Apps are great for customers, but it could be argued that they are bad for many traditional businesses that are finding it hard to move with the times and change their business models. A good example of this is the transportation app Uber. Uber is an app that seamlessly connects taxi cabs to passengers. When you request an Uber, it locates the nearest available car, tells you how long you'll wait, and gives you a price estimate. It lets you know what your driver will look like, and after your journey you rate the driver and the driver rates you! The outcome is very effective, since you both know that you are going to rate each other and the result of that rating will have implications for both of you – the driver in his ability to get future passengers and the customer in his ability to get future taxis. It leads to an almost co-created standard of behaviour and conversation that is quite cool! We'll talk about measurements later, but I think what Uber has done with rating, very similar to what eBay does with buyers and sellers, is the way the world is heading and needs to go, so that it's not just a one-way street. In many other transactions there is a duty on both sides to behave appropriately. One can think not only of taxis and passengers, but restaurants and diners, hotels and guests, and countless others transactions. At some point in the future we could be walking around with a virtual passport that would rate us on how good a customer we are, which would allow us access to preferential treatment!

I like Uber and so do millions of people around the world. Who doesn't like Uber? Taxi drivers in London and many other major cities around the world. In fact, the London cabbies effectively shut down London in 2014 by blockading major roads in protest at Uber, an act that I think served as its own goal, as it irritated most of the people in London and acted as an advertisement for all the people who had never heard of Uber. I'm sure the cabbies have some valid technical arguments, but the reality is that Uber is a thoroughly modern digital business that exists because it solves a customer issue – getting transportation. In a very mature market, Uber has managed to succeed because it does what customers want. They have created value by focusing on customer demand. And they've done it without owning one single taxi – simple, really! The cabbies might dislike this, but in reality it is impossible to stand in the way of such a customer-focused business, and the only answer for traditional businesses is to focus on the value they deliver to customers.

The March of Real Personalization

The last factor to mention in terms of technology and its impact on customer power is the role of customer data and personalization. Over the last 10 years, consumer technology has learned our names, where we're located, what we're interested in, what we buy, what we don't buy, and who we're connected to – both socially and implicitly.

With the advent of the Apple watch, a mass-circulation product that is physically connected to customers, even our feelings will become data that can be accessed. This is potentially the age of truly personalized products and services. However, I see this as a bit of a double-edged sword. From a customer's perspective, there has always been a desire to be recognized as an individual and receive solutions that relate to you specifically. This has traditionally been very difficult for organizations because the systems did not exist to store the data required, but now there is an expectation building in the minds of customers that this can be done, and more importantly, examples where it is being done. This is especially the case with the newer tech-driven businesses. For example, I enjoy cycling and I use an app called Strava, which is free. Strava clearly knows who I am, but because I sign in through Facebook, it also knows who all my friends are, a Facebook click away. Through GPS, it knows where I am and how quickly I'm cycling and how much effort I'm putting in. It also knows how many other Strava users have ridden same route, how quickly they did it, and my performance in relation to them. Because of this, it can provide me with the relevant data that I need, at the relevant time, on the relevant device that I'm using. It can therefore also start to use the data to predict my behaviour and send me relevant information to inspire me to do better and achieve my goals. To me, that is a personalized service, and because I'm comfortable releasing my data, I gain added value in return.

Compare that with one of the banks I use, which continually gets my name wrong on statements. That's what personalization used to mean, and organizations still got it wrong. Now customers' expectations are at a totally new level. However, it could be argued that this data revolution, often referred too as 'Big Data', is an opportunity for organizations to wrestle back some of the power that is now in the hands of customers. I have painted a picture of customers being able to decide what they want, when they want it, and how much they want to pay for it. In this scenario, organizations are reactive and chasing around after customers in a bid to make them happy. I imagine the hope for 'Big Data' is that it will allow organizations to be more proactive, get ahead of customer expectations, and lead customers to products and services. I suppose the best example of this is Amazon's personalized pages, which effectively say, "I know you and what you buy, I know others like you and what they buy, so here are our recommendations." There are more complex versions of this, but I'm yet to be convinced. Why? First, I have never bought anything through my personalized Amazon page, although I have purchased individual product recommendations. But I suspect that the answer to this question comes down to different individuals and generations. Though I've yet to see how the clamour for 'Big Data' will be able to tip the changing balance of power toward customers.

In conclusion, technology has become an integral part of our lives, much more than we could have ever predicted. However, the most important factor is that technology has been integral in tipping the balance of power back from large organizations toward customers. People talk about every industry being in a disruptive state due to digital advances, but I believe it's all about customers and their shifting expectations – which are now powered digitally.

2. The Global Recession

In early 2008, the latest global recession began, caused by the sub-prime mortgage crisis that hugely impacted the banking sector. In the UK, this was the deepest recession since World War II and has had implications for all parts of society. At the time of this writing, in 2016, we are gradually emerging from this recession, and the world is definitely a different place. One of the impacts of a recession is it naturally impacts consumer behaviour, not just for the period of the recession, but for a significant amount of time afterward.

Most commentators say that the result of a recession is that consumers buy less and shop for cheaper items that help make ends meet. This is generally true, but I wondered if this recession would be slightly different due to the different technological environment in which we were living. In late 2009, I read a fascinating article in the *Harvard Business Review* written by Paul Flatters and Michael Willmott, called "Understanding the Post-Recession Consumer." The article was a far-reaching piece around current consumer trends following a recession; how some would continue and maybe even become 'super-charged' and others would fall away. Three factors struck me as being highly significant and time has proved them to be true and indicative of the changing relationship between organizations and their customers. These are: demand for simplicity, mercurial consumption, and discretionary thrift.

The Demand for Simplicity

The theory is that the time of pre-recession was a time of economic 'boom' and everything had a million 'bells and whistles', multiple product features, and increased complexity. This started to change just before the recession, as consumers began desiring simpler products and services. The exemplar of this had been – and still is – Apple. Apple products are beautifully simple in both design and function and this had paid dividends with customers. Nowadays, consumers no longer accept unnecessary complexity in products or services and will penalize organizations that make them go to unnecessary effort. I think that the simplicity and low-effort requirement are inextricably linked to the value that consumers now place on their time. *The value of time is now as important as the value that money has always been*, and drives different behaviour and decision making. Simplicity often means easy, and easier often means quicker and saving time.

Mercurial Consumption

The second trend that was interesting was something that Flatters and Willmott called 'mercurial consumption'. This worked on the basis that consumers were not only agile, but also fickle. Consumers were more informed and therefore more able to make informed decisions. This was a trend that definitely will continue to dominate buyers' behaviour, especially with the ubiquity of online marketplaces like Amazon. How many people have gone to Amazon looking to buy a particular product and, having found it, scrolled down to the offending part of the page: "What other items do customers buy after viewing this page?"

Not only does this section list products bought after viewing the originally intended product, but also provides information on price and customer ratings. What if the price is better for a product with similar customer ratings? Or there is another product at a similar price with better customer ratings? Suddenly what would have been a very simple purchasing journey – I want one of these, they have it, the price is good, and I want to buy it – has become a fully informed market review. What this suggests is that people have embraced the opportunity to search around, especially if it is easy. As Jeff Bezos, CEO of Amazon, says, "We don't sell things, we enable customers to make purchase decisions."

Discretionary Thrift

The last trend was my favourite both in terms of what it meant and what it was called: discretionary thrift. This concept states that in a recession, consumers 'tighten their belts' and buy less and buy cheaper things. What Flatters and Willmott suggested was that not only will consumers have to be frugal to cut back, but even those who do not need to do so will take pleasure in doing so. This trend has played out absolutely, with customers who would not normally be frugal, let alone be proud to broadcast it, *now wearing their thriftiness as a 'badge of honour'*. If you throw into the mix the search for value, not just cheapness, you have a heady mix of change in consumer behaviour that can devastate any industry.

Nowhere has this been played out better than in the supermarket business in the UK over the last five years (2010 – 2015). The UK grocery market is dominated by four large, mass-market supermarkets (Tesco, Sainsbury's, Morrison's, and Asda). Outside of the big four, there is one significant upmarket grocer, Waitrose, and then the discounters at the 'other end', namely the giant German businesses

Aldi and Lidl. Throughout this period, there were already significant changes in buyer behaviour taking place, such as the switch to online shopping and the rise of convenience stores due to people wanting to do smaller shopping trips more frequently. The big supermarkets were on top of these trends, investing heavily in both, and aware of the impact that a recession might have with customers wanting to save money. However, they felt protected since they had diversified their own label ranges and provided for the economy end of the market. Meanwhile, Aldi and Lidl have been operating in the UK since 1990 and 1994 respectively and had been growing steadily, if unspectacularly. They were commonly known as cheap stores selling unusual brands to hard-up people, and they really weren't too much of a concern to the big four until the recession.

It wasn't just the price that worked in the favour of the discounters, but all the changes in consumer behaviour. First, due to Mercurial Consumption, customers who would have never set foot in an Aldi or Lidl felt able to give it a shot. When they did, they found it was a slightly unusual shopping trip and certainly different to any that they were used to, with strange brands and unusual products. Also, it was almost universally cheaper. But the key factor was that the products not only performed better than expected, but also that they performed as well as the products offered elsewhere. This is where the desire for value kicks in. If you can buy a cheaper product that performs just as well as a more expensive one, which one is providing you with the most value? So having tempted customers to try them and the customers discovering that it was better than expected and good value, how could customers be encouraged to return? This is where 'discretionary thrift' kicks in.

Previously, certain sections of society would have required a balaclava to shop in a discount store, and if they met anyone that they knew they would deny having ever been in that shop before! However, discretionary thrift suggests that now, if shoppers can discover value, they are proud to shout about it and are certainly not embarrassed to be associated with it. At the same time, Aldi and Lidl were very clever. They decided to compete 'head on' on quality and on product categories that potential customers valued; for example, wine and champagne. They entered their products into food- and drink-taste competitions, often winning or being highly commended. The discretionary thrift factor went into overdrive, with customers not only throwing away their balaclavas, but now openly endorsing the products and the company at dinner parties across the country … people were proud to say they shopped at Aldi because it no longer said they were 'frugal' – it now said that they were smart and savvy shoppers, and who doesn't want to be one of those? And all the stores' advertising now reflects this too.

Another factor that is often overlooked in the rise of the discounters is simplicity! On average, the big four supermarkets stock about 30,000 different products, where as the average Aldi/Lidl stocks only around 2,500. This makes a difference because not only is the shopping journey significantly more straightforward, but also running the shop becomes much easier. I spent a reasonable amount of time walking around discounters to understand their customers' experiences, and it was the simplicity that always struck me. If you are going to buy tomato ketchup, you are choosing between two products and not 52! Suppliers have driven lots of complexity into the product market on the basis that customers require more choice, and I'm sure that is true, but it's interesting that companies offering more limited choice are being more successful. It's all about finding the intersection between choice, customization, and simplicity.

So what have been the implications of Aldi and Lid, and this shift in consumer behaviour, and their ability to ride the wave of change? Well, they have basically disrupted the grocery market in the UK forever. Over the last three years, their combined market share has almost doubled from 5.4% to 9.3% (October 2015), which is unheard of in such a mature market. And recently Aldi overtook

Waitrose as the sixth biggest supermarket in the UK. Both organizations are currently recording double-digit sales growth in an industry that's growing at 1%, at best. Most of the market share that they have gained has come at the expense of the big four, which has given them all significant problems in such a low-growth and low-margin industry, which means that their bottom-line profits have been severely impacted. The reality is that no one saw this coming and certainly not on this scale. The bad news for the supermarkets is that a recession doesn't just change consumer behaviour in the short term; it's a long-term change and can even affect generations. So it's not a question of 'batoning down the hatches' and hoping for the best, but how to survive in this changed environment and, more specifically, how to add value to draw customers back.

The recession has changed consumer behaviour forever, and the triple threat or triple opportunity, depending on your outlook, of Demand for Simplicity, Mercurial Consumption, and Discretionary Thrift are at the forefront of this change. Understanding and predicting changes in customer behaviour in this fast-changing world have never been so important … it would appear that *businesses can be built and destroyed in the blink of an eye by understanding or misunderstanding what customers want and how they will behave.*

Customer Demographics

We have established that customers have greater knowledge and a voice like never before, enabled by the advances in technology and the digital revolution. At the same time, the macroeconomic world has caused consumers to think and behave differently and leverage the 'power' afforded to them by technology to search for both value for money and value for time. An already dynamic, confusing, and fast-moving picture for organizations gets a helpful overlay when we consider the impact of current demographic change.

In general, people are living longer. This means that we have an unprecedented number of generations coexisting on the planet at the same time. Fifty years ago, that would have been less of a problem, as one generation pretty much looked like the one before. The pace of change over the last 30 years means that each generation appears to face a completely different set of social, economic, and technological factors to shape and drive values, opinions, and behaviours. In fact, the 'half life' for these changes is getting shorter and shorter.

What are these generations and what are their attributes? Although the generational groups are generally agreed upon, the names are sometimes different!

1) **Baby Boomers** (my favourite term) were born between the end of the Second World War and the early 1960s. These people are traditionalists. They lived to work, as work was an important part of their lives and defined them in many ways. Often when they started their careers, they would expect to be in one job for the duration of their careers. Conservative in their outlook and trusting of authority, they believe in accumulation of wealth and did very well from home ownership.

2) **Generation X** was born between the early 1960s and the early 1980s. In the UK, this group was dubbed 'Thatcher's children' … and I am one! They have a slightly different approach to work – more 'work to live', so work is seen as a mechanism to allow them to live their lives. They have often had several employers and therefore less loyalty to them. They still believe in asset accumulation, but they suffered with the housing bubble bursting and the end of endowment mortgages, which led to an element of cynicism and scepticism with the world. They are influenced by the start of the technology revolution, but have to work hard to understand it.

3) **Generation Y, or Millennials**, were born between the early 1980s and 2000. Lots of research has gone into understanding the youngest of the current consumer generations. They appear to have a completely different attitude to life shaped by technology. They are characterized by 'live then work', which represents the fact that they are more interested in living life than working, and will work only because they have to! They are the first truly 'connected' generation, and understand and value their network. They are 'social media' savvy and use it to communicate with their network, not just for fun, but to solve problems and understand the world they live in ... they need the flexibility to connect. They do not value the accumulation of wealth and status, but are instead a generation that is all about collaboration and sharing. They also genuinely care about the world and the environment and protecting it for themselves and future generations.

4) **Generation I, born post-2000**. This group are not yet consumers, but influential in what is purchased. They are true 'digital natives', having been born into a world of smartphones and tablets ... to stop a baby Gen I from crying, you don't give it a dummy or a cuddly toy, you give it an iPhone with Moshi Monsters on it! These kids are immersed in technology – everything should have a touch screen, be voice-activated, connected to the internet, and able to show their favourite TV shows on demand! It is yet to be seen how these digital natives will develop as consumer or global citizens, but it will be interesting!

Clearly there is a significant degree of generalization included in these descriptions and there will be 'bleeding' at the edges of each grouping. However, there are clearly very different groups operating in the commercial environment. Why does this matter? First, these people are both customers and also employees. However, their expectations and desires are completely different. Perceptions of how they should be served by organizations, and how they should serve, are completely different as well. This has huge implications for all organizations, especially if they want to or have to appeal to a cross-generational population.

In terms of customer service delivery, this is incredibly important. Consider one of the simplest tasks: communication across the generations discussed. We have moved from face-to-face, postal mail, telephone, email, and texting to tweeting, posting, and Skyping. Each generation will have its preferred mode of communication and it's quite possible that an organization will have millions of customers in each generational group, with different expectations of how they want to be communicated with.

Now expectations of when and how things will be done have changed. Not long ago, it was entirely acceptable to send a letter to an organization and not receive a reply for a week. That expectation changed with email, where a day seemed a more reasonable expectation for a response ... but many organizations are still struggling to achieve that, even today. If you overlay tweeting and posting, the expectation is that a response will be almost instantaneous ... this is not excellent service, but just what is expected. I often call my young children, currently eight and twelve, the 'Now Generation', and they want what they want now and are not prepared to wait ... if one organization can't deliver something immediately, they'll find someone else who can.

Every year in the UK, The Institute of Customer Service runs a national customer satisfaction survey, asking hundreds of thousands of customers for their feedback on hundreds of organisations. This survey is called the UK Customer Satisfaction Index (UKCSI). Interestingly, it was shown that satisfaction with levels of service decreases as you pass down the generations, with the Baby Boomers being the most satisfied and the Gen Ys the least (see *Figure 1* over the page). I believe that this is a direct consequence of increases in expectations and the difficulty organizations have in meeting them.

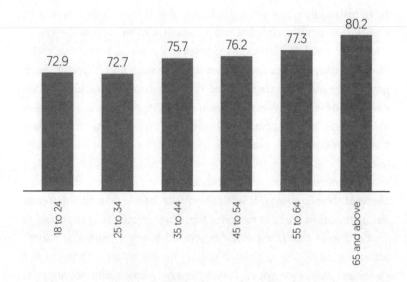

Figure 1: UKCSI Score by Age Group

UKCSI score by age group illustrates the decreased
levels of service satisfaction among generations.

What this all means is that it has never been so important to understand your current and future customers and, with this in mind, products and services will be designed to meet customers' expectations. Where there is a multi-generational customer base, flexibility and choice will be offered to set and execute the most demanding of standards. I once saw a presentation from a company called Flywheel, which was doing extensive studies into the attitudes and preferences of Gen Y, the 'y-tail' program. They asked more than 600 Gen Y customers about the brands that they love and those that they hated. Ninety-five per cent, one of the highest 'love' ratings, indicated that they loved Amazon. Amazon does exactly what the 'now' generation wants: it gives access to great choice, makes it extremely simple to buy, delivers quickly, and rarely gets it wrong. This meets the expectations of a demanding Gen Y perfectly.

However, according to this survey, only 51% of Gen Y loved Apple and 49% didn't. I found this hard to believe, but when they dug deeper, they found that the issue had to do with flexibility. Apple is famous for having an attitude that is a little bit 'our way or the highway'! They make it difficult for third-party software programs to operate with their operating systems and famously do not allow for any USB interactions with their mobile products. To an older generation that respects authority that is acceptable – but to a younger generation that craves flexibility and collaboration that sort of behaviour could be perceived as a turn off. Now I know that Apple has probably sold billions of iPhones to Gen Ys, but the study suggests that even the greatest companies in the world are fallible if they don't connect their strategy to segments of their customer base. It comes as no surprise, then, that the new Apple MacBook includes a USB for the first time. The power is tipping toward customers, and organizations upset them at their peril.

Implications of the 'Perfect Storm' of Customer Management

Hopefully, we can now all agree that this is an unprecedented time in the relationship between organizations and their customers. Technology and the digital revolution have given customers a voice like never before. The recession has charged a significant change in consumer behaviour that sees customers exercising their power in different ways. The generational demographic environment means that expectations vary significantly between generations, with the Gen Y population being more demanding that any group previously.

I believe that the implications of these factors on organizations are tremendous and many are already starting to creak under the strain.

First, there are the implications that this has on brands. I once read somewhere that brands are dead. Clearly, that is not the case; however, brands are no longer purely what the marketing function creates and pushes, a *brand is now as much about what customers are saying about it as it is about what the marketing team says about it*. Equally at a more micro level, in an age of customer reviews, the performance of any product or service stands on what customers say about it, not what the adverts say. Apparently, as a result of the 'United breaks guitars' video, United had to cancel a multi-million pound advertising campaign, as what they wanted to say was totally at odds with what customers were saying … the messages must now be aligned.

Let's consider again our example of shopping on Amazon and being drawn to possible alternatives. This example indicates the falling value a brand holds compared to the price and strong customer reviews of an alternative in a commoditized market. However, if that brand is reinforced by positive and consistent customer experience, the brand is strengthened and can stand out from the competition. It will be seen as adding value and may even on that basis be able to command a premium price. For that reason, the customer experience has never been so important. One of the safest ways of navigating these turbulent waters is with a strong brand that is very clear about what it needs to be for its customers. Link to that products and services that do what they are supposed to do and deliver value for customers and support that with a seamless end-to-end customer experience, and there is a good chance that the organization will prosper (see *Figure 2*).

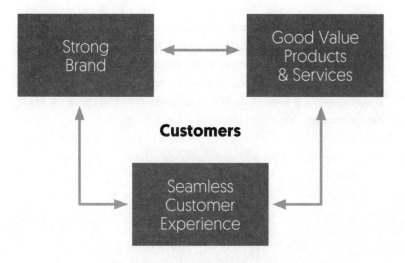

Figure 2: The Cycle of Customer Centricity

Organizations that provide products and services that
perform well and offer a seamless customer experience
will stand out from the competition.

All the organizations that are currently thriving from their customers' perspective understand that relationship. However, the 'cycle' will not work as well if the ball is dropped on any one of these factors and customers will erode the effectiveness of the brand's message. To put it another way, you can now only have strong brand if you have value driving products and services and get the customer experience right.

Customer Experience Is a Modern-Day Battlefield

For all of these reasons, customer experience is becoming the modern-day battlefield, a true differentiator that is difficult to imitate, and everyone wants a part of. However, we've gone past customer experience ... the most enlightened organizations are now talking about customer relationships ... relationships are the new (old) game in town! (see *Figure 3*)

Figure 3: The Evolution of Customer Focus

Customer relationships – creating an emotional connection between customers and the organization – are the differentiator among successful organizations.

Ten years ago we were talking about customer service. This was very transactional, like every time you called a call centre or went into a retail store. There may have been a good or a bad transaction, but the customer experience was the culmination of all these transactions. It only took one poor transaction to impact the whole experience, so there was a real requirement to get basic transactions right consistently to support the customers' experience. In the same way, the customer relationship is the aggregation of all the experiences that a customer has with a brand over time through all channels, both passive and active, including other customers' experiences of the brand. Establishing a strong relationship with customers is what drives deep loyalty and that is the differentiation that most organizations desire. Building a relationship is about creating an enduring emotional connection between the customer and the organization. I like to think of it as a bucket; when a customer starts a relationship with an organization the bucket is empty, and the objective for the organization is to fill that bucket with lots of lovely positive experiences. The fuller the bucket is, the more positive the relationship between the customer and the organization is. However, there are horrible negative experiences, and every time there is one of those it creates a hole in the bucket through which the positive experiences will start to leak. The objective is to fill that customer relationship bucket by maximizing positive experiences and minimizing negative ones and the more positive experiences there are in the bucket, the more chance there is of surviving negative experiences. Customers are more likely to forgive the odd negative experience from an organization with which they have a positive relationship ... or a very full bucket! As Warren Buffett once said, "It takes 20 years to build a reputation and five minutes to ruin it. If you think about that, you'll do things differently."

A great example of this is the UK bank, First Direct. They are a phone and internet bank and part of HSBC. They are regarded as the best bank for customer experience in the UK, backed up by the fact that they came first in the 2015 UK Customer Service Index and in the Nunwood/KPMG Customer Experience ratings. Their customers really love them … we will investigate later in the book how they do it! However, late in 2014, they implemented a new secure system for accessing accounts over the internet. Unfortunately, the system was very complex and many customers found it difficult to use and they let the organization know it on social media. For many organizations, there would have been no way back because their bucket was not full enough. However, because of First Direct's amazing relationship with their customers, they were able to work hard to fix the issue and still retain their place as the UK's number-one brand for customer experience.

Despite the power of the customers, why is it still possible to experience poor service so often? As I mentioned earlier, I believe that excelling in customer experience is like a religion; in order to make it really happen, the whole organization has to believe in it, and that's what makes it like a cult. The reality is that there are still many non-believers or partial believers, and unfortunately, belief must be absolute in order for organizations to focus first on customers when all the other pressures of running an organization would tempt them to focus on other things. Focusing on customers seems simple to achieve, but it's far from that, which is why we need to understand how the organizations that achieve it do it!

There Is a Joy in Simplicity

Although customer power is increasing, not all customers realise it yet! There is still an apathy toward organizations that means poor service is tolerated. This is particularly so where the barriers of switching to an alternative product or service are perceived to be high, and significant effort would be required from customers to switch to an alternative, which may or may not be better. That is why so many of us are still with the same bank that we originally signed up with when we were kids. We don't love our bank, and although I've heard that there are some quite good ones out there now, can I be bothered to change and isn't it better with the devil I already know?

This may be a generational thing; the younger generations are more demanding, less tolerant of poor or even average service, and feel empowered to do something about it. For those organizations that don't have the religion and feel that they are doing fine without it, beware, your days may be numbered! Barriers to entry are being shifted and removed all the time in different industries, and no matter how safe those businesses may feel now, once those barriers are removed, all that is left is the relationship with the customer. If the relationship has not been nurtured and cared for, then it will leave the organization very vulnerable to attack from the competition.

CHAPTER FOUR

Who's Good
and Why?

So far, I've made a big deal about the growing power of the customer and that there has never been a time where it was more important to focus on the customers as a sustainable business strategy. Having said this, there are still businesses delivering a very poor level of service and getting on just fine. This is backed up by the latest data from the Institute of Customer Service's recent UK Customer Satisfaction Index survey, which shows that satisfaction with service has been falling for the last few years (see Figure 4).

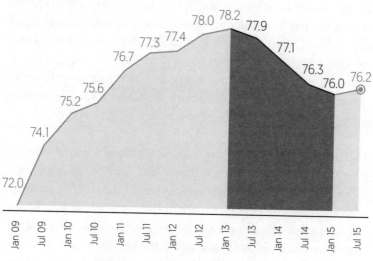

Figure 4: Overall UKCSI Over Time

The UK's recent Customer Satisfaction Index survey shows the decreasing satisfaction with customer service over the last several years.

How can this be the case, if customers are growing more important? Unquestionably, many organizations don't get it yet and continue to offer a level of service that's just not good enough. But there is the issue of what does 'good enough' mean now? I believe that customers' expectations are increasing with time. So even though many organizations have realized that they need to improve their customer experience, they are not improving fast enough to fit with the expectations of customers. If this is the case, then what is driving this increase in expectation?

The Bar Has Been Raised

Although most organizations don't get 'it', there are clearly many that do, and we've named a few of them already: Amazon, Apple, Disney, Metro Bank, and First Direct. There are also all of the new digital businesses, whose reason for existence is to serve customers and make their lives easier by solving their problems. These organizations have 'raised the bar' and made it difficult for others to keep up. Customer experience does not exist in silos. The expectation set by one organization in one industry can set expectations for other organizations across other industries, especially if the organization setting the standards is a ubiquitous one.

The best example of this is Amazon. As we found with the Flywheel survey, in Chapter Three, most people love Amazon. In most countries where they operate, they rank as one of the top five providers of customer service, and that is certainly the case in the UK. I know this from personal experience of having run hundreds of workshops and presentations where I have asked delegates to name a company that is great at customer experience. On the whole, everyone loves Amazon! Why? Predominantly, because they do what they say they'll do, all of the time, and when it goes wrong, they're great at sorting it out ... that's it! It's simple: when an organization can deliver on its promises with such regularity and keeps its customers informed with such efficiency, it raises the bar for everyone. So if a business can't deliver a parcel exactly on time, or their engineer doesn't turn up on time, or it takes weeks to process a refund, or the website occasionally crashes, or they never let you know what's going on with your case or your order... then they're not doing well enough, because Amazon can do all of that, all of the time!

So the bar is raised and for now it's up to organizations how and whether they choose to respond. As mentioned earlier, if you asked the CEOs of top organizations from around the world if focusing on customers was a good thing, 99% of them would say, "Yes" So what separates those who say it – and believe it and make it happen – from those who only say it? I believe that some of it comes from the type of business and the industry they're in. If we look again at the latest UKCSI, but through an industry lens, it is retailers, both food and non-food, that top the ratings. In fact, retailers have topped the ratings ever since the UKCSI was ever published … and it's pretty much the same story all around the world. Conversely, utilities are the laggards, and again that has generally always been the case. What makes one industry so good and the other so poor?

Why Retailers Need to Build Loyalty

There are many reasons for this, but the key is that in retail markets it is easy to switch from one company to another. At Sainsbury's, I used to say, as someone drives down the road they can turn one way for Sainsbury's and the other for Tesco. So a retailer is always thinking, "What can I do to make sure the customer comes back to my shop next time?" It's all about building a relationship with customers and keeping their loyalty. It is no surprise that retailers created loyalty cards to reward people for coming to the store, but also to encourage them to return. Loyalty cards, when used well, create a 'sticky' relationship with customers, where they believe that they are being rewarded for their loyalty. And at the same time, the customers are giving up some of their data in the hope that it improves their shopping trip, but also improves the offers they receive.

Whereas for a utility company, the customer gets little or no choice, so treating the customer well and trying to foster a deeper relationship is a waste of time and effort. I'm not saying for a second that the people at the top of utilities companies don't want to do right by their customers; I'm sure they do. But *the difference between being good enough occasionally and being the best is like an ocean.* The reality for most utility companies, at present, is that being just okay with customers, and being good at other parts of the business, are enough. That is just not the case for many other businesses and certainly not for retailers.

There are a number of other factors that make retailers focused on customers. First, there are low barriers to switching in retail, so it is fiercely competitive. A friend of mine described it as a *'knife fight in a phone box'*, and I think that says it all. The competition is effectively in real time, with so many different shopping trips happening every day, so retailers are constantly fighting for their share. Any shopping trip they can turn their way from a competitor is a victory. Retailers need to focus on keeping their customers, and maybe stealing some else's, every minute of every day. Achieving customer loyalty is essential for retailers, so by definition, most retailers are customer-focused. But, in order to be customer-centric, where the customer is truly at the heart of the business, they must go one step further. They must focus on what really matters to their customers and get those right, whether it's pricing, product availability, or the environment that customers shop in. Regardless, maximum effort is put forth to improve things for customers.

In 2011, Sainsbury's launched a new initiative called Brand Match. The way it works is that once at the checkout, the system works out how much the customer's branded products came to and compares them to the same brands at other supermarkets. If the customer's branded purchases at Sainsbury's came to more than what they would have paid for the brands elsewhere, the system issues a voucher that gives the customer the difference in value to use on their next trip to Sainsbury's. If their shopping at Sainsbury's cost less, they still got a voucher saying how much money they had saved at the shop. Interestingly, at least initially, customers receiving the 'congratulations, you've saved money today' voucher were disappointed that they hadn't been given money off, even though that would have meant that they'd spent more money initially! It's amazing how the mind craves money off. The purpose of the initiative was to say to customers that they were secure shopping at Sainsbury's, as the price was the same as anywhere else, and where it wasn't customers would get their money back. In this incredibly competitive environment, they spent millions of pounds to negate price advantage, in order to compete on other factors such as quality and service. This system was truly revolutionary.

What Attributes Make Retailers Customer-Focused?

Another attribute is speed. The whole Brand Match initiative took 10 months from inception to rollout, and that included an extensive four-month trial in Northern Ireland. In most industries, that sort of initiative would take years to get off the ground, if at all. Sometimes even after a substantial trial, the results are not always conclusive, and the decision makers have to decide, 'does this feel like the right thing to do for customers?' In the case of Brand Match at Sainsbury's, the consensus was 'Yes'. In many other organizations, I'm sure the answer would have been 'No'.

To create value for customers in the competitive and focused retail market, it is imperative to move fast in order to create the advantage for as long as possible. Because one thing is for sure: the competition will respond as quickly as they can, especially if they feel an advantage is being gained. In this case, Tesco (a competing supermarket) developed their own version of Brand Match within 18 months, which had additional features that they felt were superior. This whole sense of moving at pace pervades all areas of the business. It's very much 'sooner rather than perfect' and that benefits customers, as there are always innovations being created to increase loyalty and therefore improve customers' lives.

Another attribute that relates directly to this is retailers' attitude to innovation, risk, and failure. In order to succeed in a super-competitive market, you have to create value and to do that you have to have ideas and you have to try enough of them so that you can be seen to be delivering on a decent number of them. From that perspective, retailers not only move at speed, they also 'try stuff' in the full knowledge that not all of it will work. I'd often hear the phrase, *'Test and fail to learn and scale'*, and I believe that this is one of the central pillars of retailing. At Sainsbury's, there were often so many initiatives that it was hard to keep track of them. Most were aimed at driving greater value to the customers and increasing profitability for the organization. The reality is that some of these succeeded, but many of them failed. And although that did matter, what was more important was what had been learned and how it could be used for future ideas.

Another key capability of retailers is their focus on data. Quite literally in retail, if it moves, they measure it ... which I'm sure feeds into the old adage that 'Retail is detail'. This focus in measurement could be at a macro level, where they could be counting the number and type of transactions. This information is fed into an industry analytics system run by the IGD, which provides weekly analysis of the organization's performance against the industry as a whole, or Kantar, which provides detailed periodic information about the industry and organizational performance. I'd never experienced having this type of weekly update, not only on how the organization was doing, but its relative performance against the competition.

At a micro level, we were able to analyse every one of the 25 million shopping trips into what was bought, and when, for how much, and for loyalty card holders (Nectar), by whom. This creates the most incredible 'set' of data, which can be used to improve things for customers. That could be to make sure the right products are stocked in the right stores at the right times so they are available when customers want them or understanding customers' shopping habits and preferences so they could be offered deals and discounts on products they like and frequently purchase. However, many customers refuse to have loyalty cards because of the data that it gives to that retailer and feel that it's a bit 'Big Brother'. Although that is true to some degree, it also means they are losing out on deals and value. Retailers understand their customers better than any other organizations, with or without loyalty schemes. They do this because they have the right data, and where they don't they make it their business to go and get it, using research. Understanding customers is one of the core elements of being customer-centric, and it can be argued that the more you know, the better you can be.

It would be impossible to talk about the attributes of retailers without talking about how focused they are on their people or, as we called them, colleagues. Retailing is a people-based business. Sainsbury's employs around 160,000 people and 95% of these employees serve customers in stores. The business exists to support them and it has highlighted this by calling their head offices Store Support Centres (SSC). This is an iconic gesture to remind all the very important people who worked in the SSC what they are there for. This is the same for all retailers; the majority of their employees are serving customers, so they are extremely focused on getting the right people, training them well and managing their performance, as they have the reputation of their business in their hands.

Last, being a retailer is an important attribute itself. Shops are all around us, both physically and virtually. They are incredibly relevant to everyday life. Supermarkets are even more relevant, as food is a necessity to everyone, making them high transaction places. This is even more so nowadays with the changes seen in purchasing behaviour. Customers are buying less stuff more frequently and are usually visiting a supermarket three times a week (around 150 times a year). This is why Sainsbury's has around 25 million customer visits a week. What an incredible opportunity to build a relationship with your customers. Other types of retailers have multiple touch points with their customers ... a company like Boots, a pharmacy and beauty retailer, would have around 40 interactions with customers a year, and even a department store like John Lewis would hope to see their customers 5 to 10 times a year.

All these transactions are opportunities to build relationships and add value to customers' lives. Every transaction is an opportunity to get it right, but also an opportunity to get it wrong – so consistency becomes key. If they can't do that well, there is no way they'll survive, so they have learned to be generally good at interacting with customers. Additionally, the better the relationship, the more trust and goodwill is generated between the customer and the organization. The more trust that exists, the more customers will consider buying different products and services. This has driven big retailers into other markets where they can leverage the relationship they have established with their customers through markets such as clothing, banking, telecoms, and even energy. These are all markets where the relationship and familiarity that supermarkets have built with their customers gives them an edge over the existing players – as long as service delivery is consistent over all these products and services. Compare this to physical transaction opportunities for organizations in other industries. Public transport and perhaps restaurants and leisure organizations may exhibit similar transaction opportunities as those seen in retail. But many organizations in many other industries would realistically interact with their customers only once or twice a year. For them, every opportunity really, really matters.

Who Else Knows What's What?

Other non-retail organizations are great at delivering customer experiences, too. However, most organizations wouldn't go too far wrong if they picked up the general principles retailers adhere to. Metro Bank does; they believe that their organization should work in the same way as a retail business does and even go as far as calling their branches 'stores' and have similar lavish store openings that you would have in retail. As an organization, they have a cult-like belief in putting customers at the heart of their business. They believe in creating the type of relationship with customers that retailers have, to enhance their objective of creating 'fans', not customers.

Other organizations have realized the benefits of 'thinking like a retailer'. I have stolen this term shamelessly from a client of mine, Standard Life. Stephen Ingeldew, marketing director at Standard Life, was intrigued at how supermarkets were so adept at meeting the needs of their customers, having the ability to provide the right products at the right time, in the right way. As we discussed this, it became clear that retailers possessed many of the attributes that he was considering bringing into Standard Life. If he was successful in making them 'think more like a retailer', a more customer-centric environment would be created, so we embarked on a series of workshops that managed to do this.

Amazon vs John Lewis

Although retailers work in a very similar model for the reasons mentioned above, there is more than one way to 'skin a cat' and this is highlighted when you consider two of the most highly rated organizations for customer experience, Amazon and John Lewis. We've already talked about Amazon, their ubiquity and the fact that almost everybody believes that they offer a superior customer experience. Their idea of customer excellence is to get things right, as close to 100% of the time as possible. However, a few years ago Jeff Bezos, the founder of Amazon, said that "The best service is no service." This statement caused some consternation in customer management circles, but his statement perfectly embodies how he believes that organizations can deliver value to customers. Essentially he meant that if a business can design its systems and processes such that customers have no reason to contact that organization, then that's perfect customer service! He is focusing on the fact that a significant proportion of the reasons that customers contact organizations is when something is not done or it's done wrong or because customers are not informed as to what's going on. This is commonly known as Failure Demand. Bezos postulates that if you can totally eliminate the failure demand from your organization, as well as making things as easy as possible for customers, they will love doing business with you, because they'll never need to contact you! Bezos understands the concept of Value for Time. *People value their time now as much, if not more than, their money, especially as you move through to the younger generations*. No one wants to spend more time doing something than they need to, so the customer interaction must work and work well, every time … Amazon is a champion in this. Though to make an organization work in this way, everybody must believe the vision of the leader and commit to it … everyone needs to join the cult, which does not always make the organizations easy places to work.

One famous story about Bezos is the way that he deals with significant complaints that reach him – which many do, as he makes it clear that he wants customers to contact him, openly publishing his email, jeff@amazon.com. When he receives a serious complaint, he will send it on to the senior executives whose areas it concerns with just a solitary 'Question Mark'. Apparently everyone dreads receiving the 'question mark' email. It means the system has somehow failed a customer or group of customers and Bezos wants to know why, how will the particular situation be resolved, and how the system will be resolved so this complaint never occurs again. What he is looking for is not excuses, but a customer-centric response where everyone works together to put it right, even if it costs Amazon revenue. Truly customer-centred organizations would never put money in front of solving an issue for customers. What's also enlightening is the list of what constitutes a bad response to a question mark email:

1) We don't know what caused it
2) It wasn't really our fault
3) It was within the agreed failure rate

These sorts of reasons maybe acceptable to some leaders, but not ones who are so clearly focused on customers, as Bezos is. No stone should be left unturned to discover what the issue is, one department should never blame another department for failure, it's a shared responsibility, and although I'm sure he knows about failure rates, it's no reason not to learn from an issue to stop it from occurring again. I know lots of people think the whole jeff@amazon.com is a gimmick, and maybe it is; however, how many other CEOs of huge organizations create a channel for customers to contact them so easily? Even if someone else responds on their behalf, it's their name that's on the line. To me, gimmick or not, this is customer-centric behaviour, plain and simple.

Compare and contrast Amazon's 'it just works' methodology with that of John Lewis, the world-famous department store. John Lewis is probably the most quoted company in the UK as 'the organization we would like to be like' when it comes to customer experience. I've heard companies say they wanted to be the John Lewis of banking, of housing, of healthcare, of insurance … you get my drift! In fact, I was running a training session in the north of England, where I asked, "If you could be a retailer, which one would it be?'" The obligatory answer of John Lewis came up. Clearly this was not unusual, but what was unusual was when I asked the group how many of them shopped at John Lewis, the answer was none. Why? Because, there are very few John Lewis stores in the north of England. Its reputation for excellence is so widespread that even people who have never been to one want to be like them. There are many reasons that they are so well known for service; however, the core reason is their people or, as they are called, partners. When you interact with a John Lewis partner, it is always a consistently exceptional experience. Their helpfulness, friendliness, and knowledge of their products are legendary … you never feel like you are being sold to, just informed. I would go further and say that if John Lewis was only an online business, with the same products, warranties, and customer-centric policies, it would not be as successful. Its unique selling point is their partners, their people, make them different and create a strong emotional connection between the business and its customers.

So you see that the Amazon and John Lewis models are very different, arguably at different ends of the spectrum: one is process-system centric, the other people-centric. They are both highly effective in building strong emotional connections with their customers and even with people that are not their customers. So there is more than one way of getting customers to love an organization and this is very much dependent on the industry and what customers want and expect. What these two organizations – and the entire great customer-centric organizations – share is a 'top down' commitment to do the right thing for their customers. In fact, it's more than a commitment; it's a belief so central to their values that it almost becomes a religion. Vernon Hill, the founder of both Commerce Bank in the US and Metro Bank in the UK, was very clear about how customers were at the core of Metro Bank and that is what made it different. Many customers think of customer experience as important, but very few think of it as the core around which everything else resolves!

Customer-Centred Organizations Leave Money on the Table

The difference between 'normal' organizations and ones where the customer is at the 'core' is that these companies exist to serve and do their best for customers. It is hard-wired into their DNA to the point it is almost impossible for them to make a decision that is anti-customer. This does not mean that they are not commercial; in fact, they are generally very commercial, but they just believe that focusing on customers will, over time, optimize their revenue. I once challenged the chief financial officer of Metro Bank as to how he 'squared the circle' of customer centricity and revenue generation. I was surprised by his answer, which was both clear and succinct. He said, "There's a lot of money in banking. We've decided that we're not going to make as much as everyone else in the short term, but that focusing on customers will give us benefits in the long term." I couldn't have said it better myself! You could say that Metro Bank doesn't maximize on their revenue, they optimize it with a view to creating and maintaining customer loyalty. That is a company with customers at its core... a company that has created a cult around being great for its customers.

Another example, which serves to illustrate this, is that of contact centres – the engine room that drives most non-face-to-face inter-actions and a huge industry in their own right. I recently chaired the European Customer Contact Summit in Barcelona, where most delegates were customer experience experts. All delegates were interested to learn how they could improve the customer contact experience for their customers, while reducing cost and increasing efficiency. So I told them about First Direct, the number-one cus-tomer experience company in the UK. I described the fact that when you ring First Direct, you get through to a human being, not one of these automated menus. Everyone was saying how inefficient it must be and how it must cost lots of money. This is quite possibly true, but it's one of the first things that First Direct customers quote as to why they love it. Many agreed that this would be great, but would be impossible to do in their own businesses ... even though they were spending millions of pounds implementing technologies that effectively reduced the number of customers that would contact their centres, and therefore save money. It's easy to get investment for a contact centre if it is going to reduce the cost of the centre, often regardless of the impact on customers. But this is a perfect example of the difference between organizations with customers at the core of the business, and those where customers are on the out-side. Companies with Customers at the Core (Triple C) understand what is important to their customers and find a way to deliver it. This can often involve taking a strategic approach to customer issues and reorienting the whole organization in order to deliver. Organizational structure mirrors customer demands. Other organizations would not do this.

First Direct could make their contact centres cost less, but they believe that would impact the experience for their customers and they can see the 'bigger picture' in the same way Metro Bank could make more money from all their products, but are more interested in customer loyalty and advocacy. John Lewis does not have to have such a generous refund policy, but they are more interested in the loyalty of their customers.

The reality is that if an organization is focused on maximizing profits at the cost of everything else, it will be very difficult to have customers at the core (see *Figure 5*). There is a saying that great service saves you money, and I think that is true to a point.

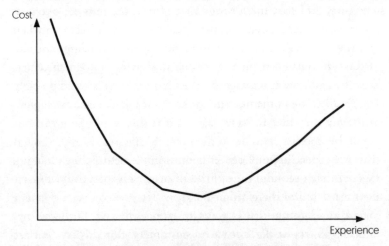

Figure 5: The Theoretical Cost/Experience Curve
Companies that focus only on profits cannot put customers
at the core of their businesses.

In the first instance, to improve service, organizations need to improve processes, procedures, and products so that customers have no need to contact them, meaning there would be fewer people and resources of the company required. This is effectively the Amazon model discussed earlier. However, once an organization has reached that point where their people and processes eliminate the 'failure demand' (very few reach that!), further differentiation costs money that won't be recovered in the short term necessarily, but will support the long-term objectives of the organization to do the best thing for its customers, with the resultant longer term benefits. Service excellence can often cost money, so be prepared to leave money on the table... truly customer-centred businesses are prepared to do that, and always do!

Customer Centric Organisations Are Not Always Easy Places to Work

Another point worth highlighting about customer-centred companies is that they are not always easy to work for. They are like cults and have challenging cultures that demand compliance with their ideology; they do not appreciate challenges to their philosophy, which often results in 'organ rejection' of those who do not to agree. In one organization it was called FIFO, Fit in or F*ck Off! Clearly, customer-centred organizations are in no way as extreme as religious cults, but they share some traits.

This was highlighted by a recent controversy surrounding Amazon, which in my opinion is one of the best examples of a truly customer-focused business. In August 2015, there was an article in *The New York Times* entitled "Inside Amazon: Wrestling Big Ideas in a Bruising Workplace." The synopsis of the article was that Amazon is an extremely challenging place to work due to its drive for continual improvement and executing new ideas. We've already discussed the 'question mark' emails that Jeff Bezos sends, but this article went further. It painted a picture of employees being treated poorly at their lowest moments by uncaring managers who were only interested in what individuals could contribute to the organization, and if they couldn't work at '100 miles an hour' then they were in the wrong place, with the strain of the environment and the culture often leaving employees in tears. It stated that, "At Amazon, employees were encouraged to tear apart one another's ideas in meetings, toil long and late (emails arrive after midnight, followed by text messages asking why they had not been answered), and held to account for standards that the company boasts are unreasonably high." What was even more surprising was that the piece was authored following conversations with hundreds of ex-employees. It's interesting because it's very cult-like behaviour. Disciples who have either managed to leave or been ejected are turning on the secretive organization to reveal it's darkest secrets and practices! One quote from one of the ex-employees was, "I was so addicted to being successful there, it was like a drug that we could get self-worth from." Take that quote and attach it to any other cult, religious or otherwise, and it would not be out of place. Sounds like something out of a best-selling novel, but it's all very real.

Even more intriguingly, and hardly surprisingly, the first people to reject the claims of *The New York Times* article were the current employees themselves! They closed ranks and dismissed the article as unbalanced and factually incorrect. One took to LinkedIn to write his response in which he said, "This particular article contains so many inaccuracies (many of them clearly deliberate), that as an Amazonian, and a proud one at that, I feel compelled to respond." He then went on to rebut most of the points made in the article, as well as stating that he, and most Amazonians, live by the 14 (!!) Leadership Principles (Number one is customer obsession … note the word choice of 'obsession'!), and that's what helps them to be their best. Again, this is quite cult-like behaviour. The current disciples reject criticism of the organization and defend living by its core values. They feel these values are totally normal and reasonable, and paint those who could not 'survive' in the environment as weak, or even liars and ridicule their claims on the basis of well, if it is that bad, how come there are so many of us are still here ... and we're doing so well?

The final piece of the jigsaw came a day later when the head of the cult, I mean organization, Jeff Bezos, had his say in a letter to all staff. In it he said that the Amazon that was described in *The New York Times* article was not one that he recognized and that he could not imagine any organization operating in such a way would be so successful in the global market place. In typical Bezos style, he invited any employee who believed they were being treated in such a way to write to him personally – at jeff@amazon.com, no doubt! He even stated that anyone working in an organization like the one described in *The New York Times* would be crazy to stay there, they should leave, and that he would leave an organization like the one described. This is exactly what you would expect: the organization leader, not calling his accusers liars, but being incredulous about the possibility of the existence of these practices. Then publicly declaring that if anyone was brave enough to own up to feeling like this, he would personally deal with the situation, and that anyone who felt that the organization was like that should really leave!

Now, I don't know which parts of this are true or not. I'd imagine that the truth is somewhere in the middle. I imagine the Amazon that is described is not one that Bezos recognizes or any of the alleged actions are anything that he has mandated. However, he has established an environment where people farther down in the organization may do things that are driven by the values he has created, that he would not approve of. What's more interesting is that even if some of the stories are not true, much of the agreed things that Amazon does are still cult like. The fact that that everyone calls themselves Amazonians, and that they live by 14 principles given to them on day one on laminated cards, is enough evidence, let alone all the talk of obsession and addiction! Nevertheless, if an organization wants to be the best, with customers at its core, then it needs to be a bit cult like. This is mainly positive; however, there may be dangers that go hand-in-hand with this, which must be watched out for.

What Is Truly at the Core of a Cult-Like Organization?

When I returned from my study trip to DisneyWorld in Florida, certain things were very clear: the role of emotions in customer experiences, the importance of leading by example, understanding what was really important to customers and meeting their needs, attention to detail and zero tolerance for errors, bringing all the team on the journey, and having a dream that everyone wanted to fulfil. I took these to every job I had subsequently and implemented them the best I could within the constraints that I had. They were more like a set of values rather than a model or 'playbook' that I operated by. The same was true when I started consulting. I could analyse a situation and decide which customer experience value needed to be instilled, and it all seemed to work.

That all changed when I went to work with Sainsbury's. I now faced one of the biggest retailers in the country, with 25 million customer transactions in stores alone, delivered through 155,000 customer-facing staff (colleagues) in the most competitive and challenging environments of them all – grocery retailing! I had to condense my thinking and years of experience of delivering 'world class' customer service into a model of operation, and I created **the 'Outside In' model of service excellence**. I refined it during my three years at Sainsbury's while testing it out against the best organizations that I found or read about. This model was formed from my observations and experience in many industries, but driven by retail. It's this model that will form the basis for the rest of the discussions in this book.

Having always valued simplicity, I wanted to and have created a model that is incredibly simple. The easier it is to understand, the easier it is to do, especially if you are going to ask other people to do it for you or with you! The model consists of 5 key elements (see *Figure 6*).

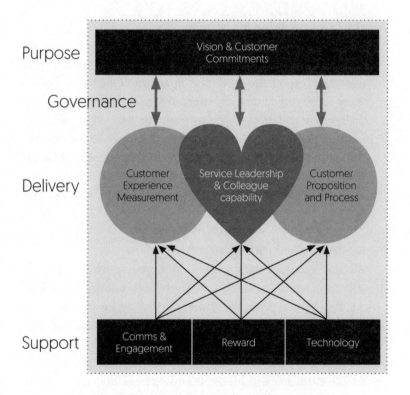

Figure 6: The Outside In Service Excellence Model

The outside-in model of service excellence incorporates purpose, customer focus, leadership and colleagues, design and execution, and governance and organization.

1) **Purpose**

   Service excellence organizations have a clear vision of what they want to be for their customers and they have values that support how they are going to 'be' to achieve it. Most organizations create a set of values; however, the difference with those that achieve service excellence is that they really live them… they are not just words on a wall.

2) **How are you doing for customers?**

   Clearly, focus on customers must be everything; however, it's imperative to know who the customers are and what it is that they want, expect and need. The organization must then believe these to be 'fundamentally true', and make them the core to their ethos and design. These must be assessed regularly to measure performance from a customer's perspective, against the things that they said were important to them. Lastly, organizations have to listen to what customers have been telling them and *understand* how they are performing for them with rigorous improvement regimes at hand.

3) **Leadership and colleagues**

   All businesses are about people. Most people have now heard about the service-profit chain. Simply boiled down, this is having a happy and profitable business by having happy customers, for which an organization needs to have happy employees. This has been widely accepted since the mid 90s and has led to a plethora of employee-engagement initiatives and projects. The service excellence organizations understand and dedicate themselves to creating the right environment to have happy employees, but possibly more important than that, develop leaders who can maintain such an environment. Leadership is everything.

4) **Design and execution**

   Consistently great service doesn't happen by accident, it happens by designing the right environment for it to happen. This comes from first looking at your processes and designing out things that don't work for customers ... I call this 'stop doing dumb stuff for customers'! Most organizations put their colleagues in difficult situations to follow processes or give answers that are crazy ... these things must be iradicated completely. The organization must then create high standards of delivery and execution – operational excellence. It's important to consistently deliver what is expected, as this develops the platform to deliver service excellence. In some organizations and industries, this is service excellence! Also, great service is created best by those who deliver it ... how much do organizations get their colleagues involved in the design of these experiences?

5) **Governance and organization**

Lastly, who makes sure all of this 'stuff' is happening? Organizations need to be organized around the customers and the objectives outlined above. This relates to commitment at the highest level, as well as the appropriate governance throughout the organization to ensure the appropriate focus on the customer is not lost. In addition to that, the best organizations are also organizationally designed to meet the needs of customers, in order to overcome the silo mentality that inflicts so many businesses and prevents true customer focus.

These are the building blocks for creating a customer-centred culture. These elements were present in all the high performing organizations that I have encountered. Missing one element leads to sub-optimal delivery for customers, especially as all elements are closely related. This is not to say that other things are not important; they are, but they exist to support the core elements. The best example of this is technology. *Technology is a means to an end, not an end in itself*, especially in establishing service excellence. I have lost count of the number of times I have spoken to companies that are keen to improve customer experience and the first action was to buy a new system or piece of technology! It's currently in vogue to buy a new

Customer Relationship Management system (CRM). I think the reason is that it has 'customer' in the title, a great wheeze by all the technology vendors! Many believe that once they have implemented the system, things will definitely get better, and maybe 'it' will all be fixed. This approach has a number of issues. First, CRM systems are notoriously difficult to implement. Even, if implemented successfully, if it is delivered without the strategic direction of the elements of service excellence, it will be completely out of context, and to employees it's just a new system. Most of these implementations, at best, have no significant impact on the organization's relationship with customers, and at worst are complete failures. Even Oracle, the big daddy of CRM system suppliers, admits that the most successful implementations of systems are within the context of an overall service strategy that incorporates all the elements of the service excellence model. Things like technology, and communications and reward are important pieces of the jigsaw, but they are supporters of the strategy, not drivers.

In the following chapters we will be analysing the elements of the Outside In Service Excellence model in greater detail.

CHAPTER FIVE

Who's Good and Why?

Knowing where an organization is going, how it's going to get there, and its culture and values while it is on the journey are fundamental to creating a service excellence model. There are inevitably lots of points on the journey where people will feel lost, not sure about what they are trying to achieve, and at this point it is important to have a clear vision and set of values that can guide them to make the right decisions and get back on course. Vision, values, mission, and purpose are always present in service excellence organizations, in the same way that they are always present in cults. They are the principles that guide everyone and bind them together in a common belief and objective. They establish the norms and should drive behaviour and consistency.

For many years, I felt that vision and values were a complete waste of time. They were just words dreamt up by the executive board and unfortunately this is often the truth. They are usually so generic and bland that they have little relevance and many people feel this way, regardless of the fact that visions and values are everywhere in most companies. But this is due to the fact that they are poorly conceived and communicated and often do not reflect the culture in the organization that people experience, as much as senior leaders like to think that they do.

I've Seen the Light!

My slight indifference toward vision and values changed when I was at DisneyWorld in Florida. Their vision and mission mean a lot to them, and it was the first place I'd been where I felt that the vision really united the workforce and I could see evidence of it doing so... *people living the vision and values as actions, not just words on a poster ...* this was incredibly powerful! At the time, the vision for Disney was 'to make people happy'. Incredibly simple and something that everyone can unite behind. It made me realize that the simpler a vision is, the more effective it could be. All the employees know that their job is to make people happy.

Think again about my story about the housekeeping staff rearranging the bears for the kids in their room. Those cleaners probably never saw those kids' faces, but I bet they could imagine what they looked like. If they know that their job is to create happiness, then they will be inspired to do things the way they did … employees buying into the vision! Happiness at Disneyland is a bright, beautiful and clean park; happy, friendly, and helpful staff; the three o'clock parade starting on time … all things that the employees can make happen if they buy into the vision, which they do.

The job of the vision is to convey a future state that the organization is striving to achieve, to create that 'North Star' towards which everyone in the organization is focused. It is supposed to be both inspirational and aspirational and bind the organization together. It brings to mind the story of when President Kennedy visited the NASA space centre in 1962 and asked a janitor, "What do you do here?" The janitor's response was that he was 'helping to put a man on the moon'! I'm not sure how true this story is, as I'm sure that when seeing a man with a mop and bucket JFK could have guessed what he was doing there, but the point is a salient one.

The role of an organization's mission is to describe what it currently does in order to achieve that vision. This should make it clearer to everyone, both employees and customers, 'what we do around here'. A good mission statement should state:

1) What the organization does
2) How the organization does it
3) Who the organization does it for

Disney called their mission the 'Walt Disney World service theme', which I really like, but it is essentially a mission: "We create happiness by providing the finest in entertainment for people of all ages, everywhere." This is the essence of why they exist, put clearly and simply so that their employees can understand it, believe it, and deliver it. It has the what, 'we create happiness', the how, 'by providing the finest in entertainment', and the whom, 'for people of all ages, everywhere'. Perfect! As well as defining for employees what they need to deliver, it also sets expectations for customers of what they will get at Disneyland, a service promise.

Disney has actually created a new mission build on the old one, but not necessarily for the better; "The mission of The Walt Disney Company is to be one of the world's leading producers and providers of entertainment and information. Using our portfolio of brands to differentiate our content, services and consumer products, we seek to develop the most creative, innovative and profitable entertainment experiences and related products in the world." Clearly this is now a mission for the whole company, but I think that even though it's a lot more detailed, it's lost its snappiness and the joy of its simplicity!

Supporting the mission should be a set of values, almost like 'rules of engagement', a set of principles that dictate 'how we do things around here'. These are sometimes from the perspective of the organization, sometimes from the perspective of the individual, and often a mix of the two. These values should reflect the culture of the organization and define the behaviours or at least the outcome of the behaviour of the employees. In Disney's case, its values include:

- Constant innovation
- High standards of excellence
- Enjoyment for all ages
- Storytelling that delights and inspires
- Inspiring trust

These 'values' fit perfectly with the mission and vision and create a compelling picture for all colleagues of what they need to achieve and what's expected of them.

My whole Disney experience forever changed my outlook around the importance of vision and values, from one of indifference to one that saw them as fundamental to success. However, it may not be necessary to have everything in the neat boxes described, even though it's pretty easy to do. What is important is having some sort of rallying cry that helps colleagues understand what they should be doing and why.

Armed with my new enthusiasm of vision and values, I sat down with the marketing team at the Pru and decided that we needed something new to help drive our strategy for our customers. It turned out to be a mix of mission and values that we called our customer promise. Quite simply we wanted to be:

- **Trustworthy** – we do what we say we'll do and never let customers down
- **Helpful** – we are knowledgeable and always try to find a solution
- **Easy** – it will always be easy to contact us and for customers to get what they need

There was a lot of debate before these were agreed on, with a push for the 'E' to be Expert rather than Easy, but we got there in the end! What was great was that these three words came to define everything we did in what would become an award-winning customer strategy … there is a joy in simplicity, and everyone could get behind it.

The best example of this was the drive to make it easier for customers to contact the business. The then-CEO, Mark Wood, discovered that the Pru owned the number 0800 000 000, and that it wasn't really being used, which he thought was a waste. He decided that in the spirit of being 'easy to deal with' we would only have one number, and that would be it. In addition, when customers rang it, there would be no IVR and they would get through to a human! At the time we had well over 250 different phone numbers servicing the business and IVRs on virtually all of them ... it seemed an impossible task ... and it was. However, over a period of three years of reorganizing the business and the systems that supported it, we managed to get down to six numbers, with none of them having an IVR ... an incredible feat that became quite well known at the time. That showed the power of a singular vision that a whole team of people understood and strove to achieve. Interestingly, when 0800 000 000 became the main default number (as it still is today), the marketing team created one of my favourite billboard ads of all time ... It was just a giant 0800 000 000, and underneath it in a smaller font '... sorry about the 8!' Genius!

The key with vision, values, and service promises is making them come alive for the employees. The easiest way to achieve this is if the words reflect what already happens in the organization; in this way they act more as an affirmation of what should be happening. This is often the case with new or start-up businesses, where the values of 'how we do things around here' evolve. As it is a small team, new members experience these being 'lived' rather than just being words on a wall. As an organization grows, it will often have more layers of management and the message can start to get diluted or influenced by an individual's belief system. I was discussing this with David Carter, the head of human resources at Pret A Manger, one of the most customer-focused organizations that I have come across. They have functioned very nicely for 30 years without writing down the values of the business, partly because they are very clear on the behaviours they expect from all their colleagues: passion, clear talking, and teamwork. However, they continue to grow both in the UK and abroad, and they now feel like it's the right time to commit the values to paper, to make it easier for new colleagues to understand what they are about more quickly. I'm sure that this will work, as the values are already actions embodied in the behaviour of 8,000 people in their 300+ stores. The most important thing will be to continue to let the actions speak louder than the words.

But the reality is that most organizations are lazy! They create visions, missions, and values that are emblazoned across their websites, on posters on their walls, on laminates in their employees' desk draws, or written on the back of their security passes. They think that is enough … it is not! The whole point of having these is to shape the thoughts, actions, and deeds of every person in the organization. Simply posting them on the back of the toilet doors normally doesn't achieve that! Think of it in the context of family values. Most of us don't write down what they are, let alone stick them on posters around the house; they would most likely be completely ignored and become useless platitudes. The way to make it happen is to walk the talk and allow the children to call you out on it if, as parents, you aren't living the values … that starts to form the desired culture. Interestingly, when I was a kid, my parents didn't put any vision and values on the wall. But they did have a poem called "Don't Quit" on the wall. Now it turns out that my siblings and I are pretty resilient and aren't really quitters, but that isn't because the poem was on the wall. It was more because our parents weren't quitters, and they used to talk to us all the time about not giving up and seeing things through to the end. As a family we were living the values and the poem was a useful reminder of what was happening anyway. So it should be this way with businesses, all the mouse mats and mugs should be a reminder of what's going on all around anyway. The issue is that often this is not the case and the vision and values are unrecognizable compared to the prevailing culture and behaviour … a recipe for disaster!

How It Should Work in Practice

When I joined Sainsbury's, I saw the effort required to establish a clearly aligned business between a common set of values and a clear vision. To put it into context, as part of the turnaround of the business, the CEO, Justin King, and the leadership team had established a programme approach under the banner 'Making

Sainsbury's Great Again' (MSGA). The central part of that were the vision and values of the business, and belief that if we got that right everything would follow.

The vision was:

- To be the most trusted retailer where people love to work and shop.

This is a very simple but also a very powerful vision. It is incredibly aspirational because in order to be the 'most trusted' by customers it suggests that they feel the same way about the organization as they do about their family and friends, people they trust. Trust is the most important commodity of a great customer relationship. Recommendation is seen as the ultimate measure of a relationship, but you would only recommend an organization that you truly trust. The vision also talks about 'retailer', not just supermarket and in doing so it aspires to be the most trusted in a category that is, at the top, synonymous with great service, deliberately aspirational. Then it talks about 'love', a very debated word. Is it really realistic for people to love a supermarket? The team felt it was, and that it should not only be loved by the customers but by colleagues as well. This vision is very clear of what the organization wants to achieve and people would be able to begin to formulate how they could impact that vision.

The mission was:

- We will make all our customers' lives easier every day by offering great quality and service at fair prices.

Another classic mission through a very clear statement, which can be broken down into *what*, for *whom* and *how*? The what 'make lives easier every day", *whom* 'all our customers', *how* 'by offering great quality products and services at fair prices'. The statement declares that Sainsbury's wants to build a relationship with its customers by impacting and making their lives easier, through many means including convenience, access, product availability, and location. It also says that everyone is welcome, Sainsbury's is about universal appeal and will endeavour to have products to suit all its customers. It also says that the quality of their products will be high, as will the level of service, which would clearly drive the strategy around product development and service design. Lastly, prices will be neither high or low, but fair … great products at fair prices had been a promise of the business for many years, rooted in offering customers value for money. This shows you how much can be said in two sentences and how they can effectively drive the decision making and actions of a whole organization as long as people believe in them.

In order to further help colleagues understand how they needed 'to be' to achieve the objectives, the values played an important role.

The values were:

- We are:
  - o Trusting each other, working together
  - o Making it simpler
  - o Delivering great service, driving sales
  - o Making it happen
  - o Treating every pound as our own
  - o Cheering on progress

Each of these intended to set a way of behaving for all colleagues. Interestingly, they were more like a 'code of practice' rather than just abstract words. Neither of these are wrong, they are just different; the key is in the explanation and interpretation, because it is this that should drive behaviour. For example:

1) **Trusting each other, working together** – was all about everyone being clear about what their job was and being allowed to
get on with it. Everyone had to trust their colleagues to do their
jobs well and not to do it for them. When that happens, all
colleagues will do their part in making the business work better.
Essentially, trust is very important and it's not only between the
organization and the customers, but also between all colleagues.

2) **Making it simpler** – everyone in the organization should strive
to make things simpler for each other as well as for customers.
Everyone should strive to remove complexity where possible
from processes and decision making.

3) **Delivering great service, driving sales** – this echoes that great
service is the key purpose of the business, since the better the
service for customers, the more sales it would create. In the retail
business, service is a revenue driver not a cost.

4) **Making it happen** – the organization needs to be action ori-
ented, and people would be judged on what they had done,
rather than what they had talked about doing. This also embodied a 'sooner rather than perfect' ethos where colleagues are
encouraged to 'give it a try' in a 'test and learn' culture. Although
failure could sometimes be a by-product of this culture, it was
accepted as long as it was learned from.

5) **Treat every pound as your own** – another 'nod' to commerciality. This is not about cost cutting; it is more about spending
money wisely and using initiative. If colleagues think that an
initiative is money well spent and they would spend their own
money in that way, then that's fine … it's a value judgement and
also quite empowering at the same time.

6) **Cheering on progress** – in too many organizations, success is
all about the end goal, and until that is achieved, everything is

a work in progress. The truth is that there are always significant milestones in every endeavour and it's appropriate to celebrate those achievements as well as the end goal ... there's a lot
more of them. This keeps morale up and makes it more likely to
achieve the final desired outcome. Life is about the journey, not
the destination, and should be celebrated along the way.

So hopefully, you can see that Sainsbury's had a very robust, simple,
and clear vision, mission and values. I certainly felt so when I joined,
and I could see how everyone in the organization could understand
and get behind them. However, to avoid having these become platitudes on a wall, more was needed. I remember that I was asked to
go on the trial run of 'The Vision Programme' within three weeks of
being there. This was a repeat of something they had done five years
previously and involved taking all senior managers, everyone down
to the store manager level, offsite for two days in a series of 70 or
80 events held over a few months. The purpose of these events was
to talk about nothing except the vision, mission, and values – that
was it! All activities were geared to understanding these better and
importantly how they could be brought to life using real-life examples that happen in the business ... real-life decisions that people
have made and how they relate to the value of the business. This
'iconic' event was formulated to be both memorable and instructive;
never before had I seen such commitment to the communication
and understanding of visions and values.

It didn't end there, either. Everyone who attended the Vision Programme was expected to run a similar one-day event for their
teams, called a 'Scout Hut', because they were generally held in
Scout Huts! They were given all the tools they needed to run the
event, plus a script of how to do it, but their job was to make the
vision and values come alive for their teams in the same way that
it had been done for them. There must have been over a thousand of these Scout Huts all over the country; again, this was done
over a period of a few months. And there's even more! Everyone

who attended a Scout Hut had to then run a much shorter session with their teams, explaining the vision and values! It was the most involved and detailed cascade process that I have ever been involved in or seen.

This would have been an expensive exercise in both delivery and also in people's time. But that was the exact point:, this was something so important to the business that it had to be done, almost regardless of the cost ... you can't put a commercial rate of return on that sort of investment.

Can People Hum the Tune?

When people come and go over the years, it's important for an organization to refresh the vision and values periodically, so that the new people will 'get it'. An iconic cascade process such as this is both memorable and indicates to everybody how critical the values are. As a result, the values have slipped into everyday language and are referred to in everyday life, which is exactly what was intended.

This was also supported by a very clever initiative around love, which was changed to an acronym L.O.V.E., meaning Living Our Values Everyday ... see what they did there, brilliant! This initiative had many parts, of which my favourite was love cards. These were funky postcards that were available to all colleagues with imagery connected to love. The intention was that when a colleague saw or experienced another colleague 'living the values', they would write a message on a love card and give it to the relevant colleague. It was amazing how much they were used and how they made people feel valued and recognized ... and I know that because I received a few, and it always made me feel great.

Ultimately, the sign of success is not how many people can recite the vision and values verbatim, it's about setting up some 'rules of engagement' that will drive cultural norms of behaviour. When I was at Bupa, I once decided to find out how many people knew what the values were, and I asked people randomly about these. What was amusing was that some people knew that they were written on the back of their ID passes, so I could see people frantically trying to find them before the 'madman' (me) got to them! What perturbed me the most was not that most people didn't know what they were, but the fact that most people weren't even close. The exercise was not one of memory and rote learning, but one of general understanding. If people had been able to give me a broad understanding of the values, in their own words and as they felt them on an everyday basis, that would have been good enough. I refer to this as **being able to 'hum the tune'**, rather than being able to play all the notes and sing all the words. Humming the tune is good enough, because the values are embedded in the behaviour that exists in the organization and should be what is expected from colleagues: 'the way we do things around here'.

How Does It Work at Amazon?

Let's consider Amazon again. We have already discussed how well regarded they are at delivering an excellent customer experience and how as a result it may be a challenging place to work, as all customer-centric organizations must be due, to their commitment to high standards. We know that in Jeff Bezos they have a leader whose heart is in making his organization work brilliantly for customers. All the ingredients needed for a customer-oriented organization or a cult are there. In which case we should consider Amazon's vision statement:

> "Our vision is to be Earth's most customer-centric company; to build a place where people can come to find and discover anything they might want to buy online."

How powerful is that: Earth's most customer-centric company. This leaves no doubt for those working at Amazon what their intention is and guides their behaviour and decision making. Even the language is interesting, the use of the word 'Earth' rather than, say, 'world', indicates something bigger than most people can imagine ... they will not be surpassed by anyone and if this is ever achieved, they won't stop moving forward and trying to improve. This is a truly inspirational and aspirational vision, and also incredibly simple.

When Bezos established this vision in a fledgling company in 1994, that would have been enough, but as organizations grow, they need to state more explicitly how people need to behave. Amazon has 14 values or, as they call them, 'Leadership Principles' for the Amazonians, because everyone at Amazon is a leader. I think it's interesting what they say about these principles on their recruitment website:

> "Our Leadership Principles aren't just a pretty inspirational wall hanging. These Principles work hard, just like we do. Amazonians use them, every day, whether they're discussing ideas for new projects, deciding on the best solution for a customer's problem, or interviewing candidates. It's just one of the things that makes Amazon peculiar."

I couldn't have said it better myself ... in fact, it is what I've been saying! So what are the principles?

- Customer obsession – start with customers and work back
- Ownership – never say 'that's not my job'
- Invent and simplify – find new ways to do things, but keep them simple
- Are right a lot – good judgment, good instincts
- Hire and develop the best – each hire raises the performance bar
- Insist on the highest standards – which others might consider unreasonable

- Think big – think differently and look around corners to find ways to serve customers
- Bias for action – speed matters, calculated risk taking valued
- Frugality – accomplish more with less
- Learn and be curious – what are the new possibilities
- Earn trust – treat others respectfully
- Dive deep – operate on all levels and stay close to the detail
- Have backbone, disagree, and commit – have a voice
- Deliver results – always rise to the occasion and never settle

Wow, what a set of guiding principles. And you've got to love the first one: customer obsession! For the purpose of this book, these have been paraphrased for ease, but each principle has almost another set of behaviours to describe them. What is required to be a good Amazonian is clear and it appears to be extremely demanding. To live all these principles every day would require absolute commitment that most people would be unwilling or unable to give. But that's the thing, isn't it – great customer-centric companies are very challenging to work for, which has led to some of the issues that Amazon and others have had. You only have to bring together a few of the principles above to create a high performance culture: customer obsession, ownership, high standards, and deliver results; these on their own would create a tough organization. This is the type of culture that you need if you are going to become and remain the 'Earth's most customer-centric company'. Becoming a great customer-focused organization is actually really difficult. It requires discipline and many tough decisions. Interestingly, although Amazon has a lot of principles, when you analyse them they are not that different to the values that I outlined for Sainsbury's ... certainly, all the Sainsbury's values fit into the Amazon Principles. Clearly great minds think alike!

... and John Lewis

John Lewis stores are feted around the world for many things, which enable them to deliver exceptional service, but I think that it is all made possible by their vision statement:

> "The Partnership aims to deal honestly with its customers and secure their loyalty and trust by providing outstanding choice, value and service."

This is exceptionally clear and would be all that a partner or prospective partner would need to know. The values also support this:

- Be honest
- Give respect
- Recognize others
- Show enterprise
- Work together
- Achieve more

Many people put John Lewis' success down to its partnership model, which effectively means that the partners (employees) own the business. There is significant evidence that employee-owned businesses outperform other business models and have higher employee engagement and higher customer satisfaction. However, in the case of John Lewis, that alone does not give them enough credit for the training they give their partners, not only in product knowledge, but also into what it means to live by the John Lewis values and principles and to achieve the vision. It helps that the partners get to share in delivering the vision, but time is invested in ensuring that they know and understand what is expected of them.

... and Apple

Apple is another really good example of this. There are no signs of vision and values on their walls or their website. This doesn't mean that they don't have one, but that it is more something they live by rather than talk about. It would appear the direction is partly determined by statements from their leaders, firstly, Steve Jobs, and more recently Tim Cook at various Apple conferences.

Apple's current vision statement was introduced by CEO Tim Cook, who stated, "We believe that we are on the face of the Earth to make great products and that's not changing. We are constantly focusing on innovating. We believe in the simple, not the complex. We believe that we need to own and control the primary technologies behind the products that we make, and participate only in markets where we can make a significant contribution. We believe in saying no to thousands of projects so that we can really focus on the few that are truly important and meaningful to us. We believe in deep collaboration and cross-pollination of our groups, which allow us to innovate in a way that others cannot. And frankly, we don't settle for anything less than excellence in every group in the company, and we have the self-honesty to admit when we're wrong and the courage to change. And I think regardless of who is in what job, those values are so embedded in this company that Apple will do extremely well."

What is clear is that all employees believe what he says and live the values. Having said that, this statement has a vision, "We believe that we are on the face of the Earth to make great products," followed by a number of values or principles:

- Focus on innovation
- Simplicity
- Ownership of primary technology
- Making a contribution

- Focus on meaningful and important projects
- Working together
- Focus on excellence
- Self-honesty and humility

When I was at their head office in London recently, I asked a senior employee what defined great products and he said that it was, "Products that changed customers' lives." It was about an emotional connection between the products and their customers. Interestingly, when I asked him what it was like to work for such a successful tech company, he said, "We're not a technology company, we're a customer-experience company," a quote direct from Tim Cook. When Apple defines itself as a customer-experience company, then surely that's a lesson for everyone! It's interesting to compare and contrast these Apple values with those of Amazon. Again they are very similar, really focusing on achieving excellence, or the very highest of standards through innovation, keeping it simple, and working together. It is another organization that must be challenging to work for, due to the high standards, but also incredibly rewarding.

So how does Apple ensure that all its employees 'get it' if it is not openly explicit about its vision and values? Well, one of many things that Apple is famous for is Apple University. This is where employees of all levels go to learn how to improve their performance and ensure Apple continues to thrive. One of the courses is called "What Makes Apple, Apple." Apparently all employees who work for Apple must attend this course, normally at the beginning of their employment, but with frequent refreshers because it is imperative that everyone remembers which way is north and how they are going to reach their destination.

In many ways, Apple is one of the most cult-like of all the customer-centred companies, because not only does it do much of what the others do, but it is also incredibly secretive about what it does and how it does it. This has been the case for its products

117

and their development, but also extends to the culture and how it is created. They believe that they are different and that difference is what makes them successful. Letting everyone know what that difference is would clearly be counterproductive and would erode their competitive advantage. But we know enough, in that we know the most successful company in the world is completely focused on customers, changing their lives, and ensuring that all their employees understand "What Makes Apple, Apple" and therefore what is required of them to continue this customer focus.

... and Metro Bank

Lastly, let's consider Metro Bank again. We know how customer-centric they are, but how do they make this translate for their colleagues? Their vision is:

> "Amazing the customer means providing unparalleled customer service, making sure every transaction goes quickly and smoothly. It means fulfilling customer needs, even anticipating them. More than that, it means turning customers into *fans*. We want them to tell their family members, friends, and business associates about the products and superior services we provide."

Perhaps a bit wordy, but this bank is hell-bent on being more like a retailer than a bank, which is not an easy stunt to pull off! To Metro Bank, it is more important that the values run through the whole organization by introducing them to all employees at their 'immersion' ... most people would call it an induction, but they're different! The values have the very useful and memorable AMAZE acronym, which is used frequently by everyone in the business. Note that it is also the first word used in describing the vision. This may appear gimmicky, but it certainly helps colleagues to 'hum the tune'. If it's the only thing that colleagues remember after their 'immersion', then I'm sure that would do just fine.

Imagine a whole workforce just remembering that the only 'rule' is AMAZE the customer! They take the whole thing so seriously that their head office is called 'AMAZE Central'! AMAZE actually stands for:

- Attend to every detail
- Make every wrong right
- Ask if you're not sure ... bump it up!
- Zest is contagious, share
- Exceed expectations

I won't go into what they all mean; they are explained beautifully in the chairman of Metro Bank, Vernon Hill's book, *Fans, Not Customers*. But again, it's clear, easy to understand, and easy to remember ... and, surprise surprise, completely in line with other cult-like organizations. This is fundamental to everything they do at Metro Bank and it's imperative to them that not only everyone understands it, but that everyone constantly reinforces it on a daily basis. These values are lived every day in this business. They are actions rather than words and it is this that fuels their fevered customer centricity, powerful elements for any cult.

Metro Bank's sense of direction is absolutely clear: everyone in the business knows what they have to believe in and that's a fundamental part of why they are members. They believe in the vision and agree with their behaviours, and if they didn't, they couldn't be part of the organization ... they would leave or the organization would reject them.

Vision and values couldn't be more important in setting the direction of an organization and helping establish its culture and way of being. But the reality is that although most organizations do have vision and values, it is the lengths that an organization goes to embed these into the business that matters. How much are they spoken about? How much do they drive the decision making of colleagues? How much are they just 'the way we do things around here'?

So It Works, Right?

Let's consider another set of vision and values:

- **Respect** – we treat others as we would like to be treated ourselves. We do not tolerate abusive or disrespectful treatment. Ruthlessness, callousness, and arrogance don't belong here.
- **Integrity** – we work with customers and prospects openly, honestly, and sincerely. When we say we're going to do something, we will do it; when we say we cannot or will not do something, then we won't do it.
- **Excellence** – we are satisfied with nothing less than the very best in everything we do. We will continue to raise the bar for everyone. The great fun here will be for all of us to discover just how good we can really be.

Sound familiar? It again sounds very similar to some of the others that I have mentioned. But in this case, these values were taken from the website of Enron just before it collapsed in 2001 following a series of events that included a lawsuit filed by investors and a government Investigation that led to its bankruptcy. Many top-level executives served prison sentences. I know this is an 'off the other end of the scale' example, but it demonstrates that words are meaningless, unless they are backed by honest thought, action, and deed. Being truly customer centric is easy to say, but not easy to do. It is unlikely that Enron set out to achieve what they did, but little by little they started to break their own values due to external pressures, thinking, "Just this once," and before you know it … you're making decisions against the customer, or worse, you're in jail!

During a recent conference, I spoke to Sam Conniff, CEO of the marketing agency Livity. Livity is an agency with a difference. They call themselves a Youth Marketing Agency because, as well as having a stellar list of blue chip clients for whom they provide all the normal marketing services, they also open their doors to the youth of South London, who come in and hang out and help with work projects. They work with young people every day who receive training, equipment, support, and opportunities to build brighter futures. What was really interesting was that in his talk Sam discussed how businesses with a social purpose were performing significantly better than those without it and that purpose-driven businesses were the way of the future. We got chatting afterward and both agreed that it probably wasn't just businesses with a social purpose that do better, but those with any driven purpose, especially if the purpose was for the benefit of humanity. This included organizations whose purpose is to benefit their customers, rather than to make profit. Overall, these organizations will perform better in the long term – **purpose before profit leads to sustainable growth.**

Living Values Every Day is the single biggest difference between truly customer centric businesses and those who are not. Customer-centred businesses don't make a quick buck at the expense of their customers and are often willing to leave money on the table if it means doing the right thing for customers. They do not see a conflict between being commercial vs being customer centric. Rather, they see being commercial as a long-term thing. Short-term thinking is definitely the enemy of customer centricity, and unfortunately many organizations are run on a short-term basis ... they think annually, but in reality it is often quarterly. Pressure to meet quarterly targets, revenue, profit, or costs often creates suboptimal decisions in terms of customers. Often, organizations blame their shareholders for this, which I find strange. If there was ever a group of stakeholders who were interested in the long-term health of an organization, it's the shareholders! Organizations need to stop blaming the shareholders for short-term decisions, and start focusing on the big picture.

Being customer centred does not mean that a company can do something that is 'anti' customers today because they did something 'pro' customer the day before. This is not a nil sum game. Customer-centric businesses go out of their way to create, as they call it at John Lewis, 'win-win' situations for both the customer and the organization. Even though for the organization the 'win' may not be in the short term, it can be in the long term in terms of relationship building.

Essentially a truly customer-centric culture needs to have clear purpose, vision, and mission that every single person in the organization can buy into ... a clear North Star, a guiding light. The values of the organization should then support this, making it clear that "This is the way we do things around here." Behaviours and actions in line with the values should be celebrated and those that are not should not be tolerated. But this can only happen if the values are more than words on a wall but lived every day. Can all the colleagues in the organization hum the tune?

CHAPTER SIX

How Well Are You Doing for Your Customers?

Almost every book or article that has ever been published about customer experience, customer management, loyalty, or marketing has a chapter or two around the aspect of 'know your customer'. The reason for this is because it's absolutely fundamental. Therefore I'm not going to disappoint by not including one, although I'm going to come at it from a slightly different angle.

Knowing and understanding who your customers are is vital to any business, it is the ship on which billions of pounds of research and analysis sails down the river ... not a complete waste of money but often criminally over-engineered! I believe that knowing your customers should be more of a 'broad brush' exercise than one of fine art. Often when most organizations conduct a segmentation strategy what normally gets generated is a whole set of 'personas' to help people in the organization understand better what their customers want and how they think. These are normally things like: Linda, a 45-year-old, stay-at-home mum with a husband who works away a lot, two kids and a dog, lives in a semi-detached house in middle England. The personas get so specific that they become a very small section of the population, so to compensate for that, the number of personas increases. I have seen a client who had 14 different types of personas for customers ... at which point they might as well have said that their customers were everyone!

Understanding the demographics of your customers is important, especially in designing products and service, but the trend is now toward personalization, with the re-emergence of the so-called Customer Relationship Management (CRM) systems. These systems are seen by many as the silver bullet to fix customer experience: "Once we know everything about our customers, we will be able to target products and services that are individual to them ... real personalisation." It would be great if I had a pound for every time I have heard that – I would be a rich man! The reality is that if these systems were to be delivered in the way that they were originally scoped, then it would be likely that they would improve individual customer interactions, fundamental for building an effective relationship with customers, but there is so much more involved.

What Do Customers Really Want?

As well as knowing broadly their customers, great customer-centred businesses have an acute understanding of what their customers want and need. First, they are great at listening to and understanding their customers, and second, they always know how they are performing in relation to these customer expectations. I've read in many places that the most important thing in delivering service excellence is to "exceed customers' expectations," but I don't believe that is always the case. The part of this statement that is true is that customers do have expectations and it's vital that organizations know what they are. As discussed earlier, it's the inability to meet ever-changing and increasing expectations of customers that causes a decrease in general satisfaction. So although there is a need for organizations to keep up with the best, more importantly they need to keep up with what it is their customers want and need.

At the centre of what customers want is something I like to call the 'fundamental truths'. These are core expectations that customers have and generally want an organization to deliver. Most organizations refer to these as 'hygiene factors', which as a term normally appears dismissive and almost negative. Organizations almost ignore hygiene factors because they believe these should just happen, almost not worth focusing on because they want to focus on things that 'surprise and delight customers' in order to exceed their expectations. However, you can't exceed expectations if you have not met them in the first place, and you can't get them right if you don't understand the 'fundamental truths' of what your customers expect.

When I first arrived at Sainsbury's, lots of people talked to me about the need to improve the customer experience, which was nice as that was what I was there to do. This is great because everyone has a view and everyone has an answer ... also interesting. Collectively there was a theme building, which was a need for more 'theatre' in the stores. Theatre meant more opportunities for customers to interact with colleagues and the products, things like product tasting and demonstrations, to having digital displays where people were queued to buy their shopping. Even though there is evidence to support some of these ideas and they were all interesting, something didn't ring true about it. Andrew Mann, a smart guy who was in charge of customer research, made a statement that would drive my thinking from that moment onward. He said, "Customers don't want great service, they just want good service all the time." This statement ran contrary to everything that I believed, but he had research that suggested customers just wanted us to do the stuff that they would expect us to do, do it well, and do it all the time. Somewhat begrudgingly, at the time, I thought that this made perfect sense, especially for the nature of customers' interactions with supermarkets.

There is a relationship between the number of times a customer experiences your brand, and how much you have to do to 'impress' them (see *Figure 7*).

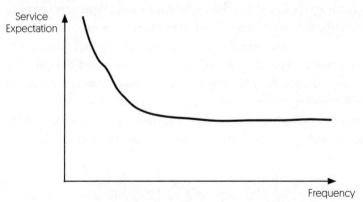

Figure 7: Service Excellence Atrophy Graph

Customers may not expect excellent service all the time,
but consistently good service.

With a high-interaction organization such as a supermarket, customers can visit a store three times a week, hundreds of times a year. In this case, what they value are the things that are supposed to happen, consistently and reliably. This is challenging for such organizations because there are many opportunities to get it right, but also many to get it wrong. Both a blessing and a curse, getting it wrong too often will result in customers switching to competitor organizations. The frequency of customer visits drops off in different types of retailing, if you consider food retailing compared with a department store like John Lewis, which may have customers who visit five times a year. There are more requirements for a 'wow' there, but they must get the fundamentals right first, regardless. This is why *exceeding customers' expectations and all this stuff around 'wow' moments can be a bit one dimensional* ... and the nature of the business itself is an incredibly important factor.

Craig Kreeger, CEO of Virgin Atlantic, and I discussed the expectations of the customer experience at length. Virgin Atlantic may fly customers with their families on holiday once a year while short-haul carriers like Easy Jet might carry their customers from five to 50 times a year. Although they are both airlines, the expectation of them is driven not only by the brand but also by the nature and frequency of transactions. The fundamental truths for both may be the same – timeliness, safety, comfort, and friendliness – but achieving this every time might be enough for Easy Jet, but unlikely to be so for Virgin Atlantic. Put another way, *you don't have to 'wow' a customer to 'wow' a customer*! Understanding customers' expectations specifically for an organization is crucial, although what customers would expect from one – to 'delight them' – will not necessarily mirror what is expected from another.

What Comprises Good Service?

So, if 'good service every day was great service', then what defines good service, and what are the 'fundamental truths' of a retail shopping experience? The great thing about fundamental truths is that they don't change that often … how they are delivered certainly changes, but not the truths themselves. Therefore, finding it out for food retailing was very straightforward, because it has been the same for more than 100 years:

- Availability – know what customers want and keep your shop full!
- Environment – ensure the shop is clean, hygienic, and easy to navigate
- Engagement – customer engagement with staff should be pleasant and helpful
- Exit – After shopping, customers want to leave quickly and easily

These factors had been the same long before I arrived in retailing and will be so for a long time to come. How they are delivered will change immensely, but what they are won't. A good example is the advent of self-service checkouts. This is technology that was invented to help customers get out of stores more quickly (theoretically) and requires little human interaction (ideally). Nevertheless, when a human is required, they still need to be friendly and helpful … it's a fundamental truth! This may seem obvious; however, I have had numerous conversations with people who didn't believe that was true! Unfortunately these people believed that the technology had changed the nature of human beings … because they are serving themselves, a cursory glance and effectively allowing the customer to continue was enough … over time, we proved otherwise.

These fundamental truths are incredibly strong. Failure to meet customers' expectation of them can lead to the complete failure of that organization. Yet they are so easy to dismiss, especially if you consider them to be 'hygiene factors'. When Justin King took over Sainsbury's, it was struggling. One of the central issues for the organization was poor availability in the stores. When customers went to do their weekly shop, they were frequently met by empty shelves. Empty shelves mean that customers are unable to get their full shopping lists and if it's an essential item, it means another trip to the shop at another time ... increased effort that no one likes. It's pretty easy to see why customers would start to desert a store if that sort of thing was happening on a frequent basis. Don't break the fundamental truths. Justin quickly acted to fix this. This makes the whole concept of having more theatre for people quite amusing. The fundamental truth was that customers didn't want to be in queues in the first place, and any money should be spent on making sure that they didn't have to be, not on entertaining gimmicks.

An organization that was executing the basics of retailing brilliantly in the 1990s was Tesco, under the stewardship of the then-CEO, Terry Leahy. As part of my fact-finding tour when I was at the Pru, as well as spending time at Disney I also got to spend some time at Tesco in Cheshunt. I was just as bowled over by their customer focus, the vision of 'Every little helps', the mission of 'No one tries harder' for the customer and the values of 'Better for customers, simpler for staff, and cheaper for Tesco'. It was clear to me then that everybody believed and lived these mantras, from the senior board to the staff at the checkouts. This very simple ideology meant that they were always focusing on the customers. They had a customer planning process that was second to none. They would listen to their customers to generate ideas for improvement, and they would execute these religiously on an annual basis. If an idea didn't make things 'better for customers, simpler for staff, or cheaper for Tesco', it didn't get done. They also focused on the 'fundamental truths' of food retailing. Tesco invented the now-standard, concept of 'one in front', whereby if there were ever more than one customer in front of another, they would open another till. Tesco knew how important this was and spent millions advertising this policy; they knew that they were making a difference to one of the fundamental truths.

This incredible focus had turned Tesco into one of the most success-ful companies in the world by the end of the 90s. Fast forward to 2016, and Tesco is a shadow of its former glory, has been engulfed in scandal after scandal, has had to replace Leahy's successor, Philip Clark (a Tesco lifer), and it is losing market share, predominantly to the discounters Aldi and Lidl.

So what has happened to this once-mighty customer champion? How could it have lost its way so badly?

There have been many theories put forward, but it is easier to listen to what Dave Lewis, the current CEO, said at a conference in November 2015, just over a year after taking over the reigns: "Customers are our magnetic North ... we lost the virtuous circle, we focused on margin, not on customers. We made some bad choices."

That says it all: they forgot that customers were the most important part of their business and they forgot about the fundamental truths. And what is this virtuous circle that he is talking about? Well it's quite simple really, and something that Tesco used to be famous for (see *Figure 8*).

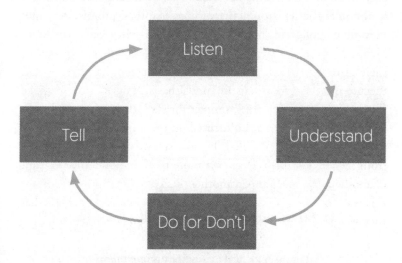

Figure 8: The Customer Experience Improvement Cycle
The virtuous circle of customer engagement: listen, understand, and act.

First and foremost, listen to your customers. Second, understand what it is that they are trying to tell you. Third, act upon what they say if it makes commercial sense in the long term; but if it doesn't, look for other ways to meet the need. Lastly, let customers know what you are doing to help them and what you're not going to do, too. This is what builds trust and transparency ... *it's not just about doing what customers say, it's about understanding what they say!* And guess what? The secret is to never stop doing it!

Building Fundamental Truths into Commitments

Every organization has some fundamental truths of its service delivery and customer experience and it's imperative to find out what they are. Delivery of these fundamental truths becomes core to the customer experience strategy, they become the 'pay to play' factors, and there's no 'wowing' of customers until they are achieved. They are the benchmark for operational excellence in the organization – get them right and everything else will follow. Many organizations create a 'customer charter' around these things that they 'promise' to do for customers, alongside, 'how' they are going to do it (see *Figure 9*).

Figure 9: Typical Customer Commitments
Delivering the fundamental truths to customers must come before any "wowing" of customers can be achieved.

These should support the values of the organization that have already been communicated.

The staple of any customer strategy is being easy to deal with and listening to customers. Today most people are time poor and therefore value their time and effort as preciously as they do their money, which creates the concept of 'value for time'. Customers now want everything to be easy, and anything that requires time and effort has to be equated against some sort of need or desire.

Making anything easier is a real competitive lever. People value the amount of effort that they have to put into something, or the lack of it, and this is driving everything to get easier and easier, with new entrants into markets leading the way, as they know that this is a way to competitive advantage. Consider the touch ID on all Apple's mobile products now. When they discovered this technology, they knew that it would give their customers time back and remove the effort of always having to enter their passcode. The amount of time saved is one or two seconds, but they understood the 'value for time' to the extent that they bought the company that made it so that it would be exclusive to their phones. They didn't know what it would lead to in its ability to now power the verification in their mobile 'Apple Pay' solution. Time is a valuable commodity to customers.

Brilliant Basics and Magic Moments

There is another term used for continually achieving the fundamental truths and that is 'Brilliant Basics'. This was a term coined many years ago by our friends at Disney. They cottoned on to the fact that the first thing that an organization needed to do was be brilliant at the basics and focus on ensuring these are delivered consistently day in, day out. However, the term Brilliant Basics has another element: 'Magic Moments'. Magic moments are the pieces of magic that create the memorable and emotional events that everyone describes as a 'wow' moment for the customer. There are whole teams tasked with creating magic moments for customers, which is great, but you cannot have magic moments without brilliant basics ... there's a reason Disney put them together!

Magic moments and brilliant basics remind me of the incredible success of the London Olympics in 2012, still held up as the best Olympics ever held in terms of customer experience. Everyone still talks about the brilliant atmosphere created by the amazing Games Makers, the thousands of volunteers who helped around the park high-fiving people and taking peoples' pictures. These are certainly the memories that people recall ... these were some of the magic moments. However, a colleague of mine, Heather McGill, was the director of customer experience for London 2012 and talked more about the 'Bums, Bogs, and Burgers'. These were some of the brilliant basics or fundamental truths that she had to get right before anything else counted. 'Bums' was getting the seats comfortable and the right size for the growing posterior of mankind! Asking customers to sit on uncomfortable seats for hours on end wouldn't lead to a great experience, no matter how exciting the sport was. 'Bogs' was all about the toilets. It's a rule of nature that people need to use the toilets and the inability to do so is guaranteed to ruin even the most entertaining event. There is also the question of timeliness here, because, 'when you gotta go, you gotta go', so endless queues or the need to be an advanced map reader to find one were out of the question ... location and plentiful supply were tantamount! Lastly, Burgers! Ever tried to enjoy anything when you are hungry? It's very difficult. Ever had to queue for hours for food when you're starving? It's a deal breaker. Making sure there were enough food stations with appropriate variety, manned to an optimal level, was essential. This gave rise to, temporarily, the largest McDonalds in the world ... which I went to on numerous occasions and even though it was enormous, you never had to wait very long. Genius! Don't get me wrong, I'm sure that there was a mountain of other things to get right, but not losing sight of the brilliant basics gave the Games Makers the opportunity to weave their magic and make it the exceptional experience that it was.

Know How Well You're Doing for Customers

So, once an organization knows broadly who their customers are and what they want (absolutely and precisely), it's time to deliver the fundamental truth consistently and maybe sprinkling a little magic dust on top!

It's essential to know how well customers' needs and expectations are being met, since this determines how they feel about and what they say about an organization. So how can an organization understand how well they are doing for customers? This is where it becomes all about the measures. Measures are a great way of aligning on organization, as what gets measured gets managed. However, measures can be extremely dangerous, too, as colleagues get pre-occupied with the measure itself, rather than what it means, especially when the measures are aligned to bonuses. So although measures are vital, they should be approached with caution.

I believe it's best to have a number of sources of understanding how well the fundamental truths are being delivered for customers, and I have developed The Customer Experience Intelligence Matrix that helps to think of customer metrics, how they have evolved, and what they are good at telling you and therefore what they should be used for (see *Figure 10* over the page).

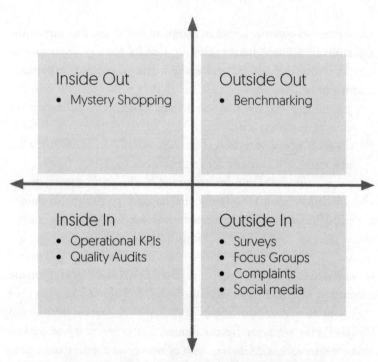

Figure 10: The Customer Experience Intelligence Matrix

The Customer Experience Intelligence Matrix measures how well an organization's fundamental truths are being delivered.

1) Inside-In Metrics

These are your traditional internal key performance indicators, often based on service level agreements created by the organization, about the organization, for the organization. These are normally based on some sort of general prediction of what customers want. A good example is turnaround times: "We answer queries in five days." The five days might, at best, have been decided due to some research, which is probably old, more often it's arbitrary or industry standard. What then happens is that another arbitrary figure is overlaid on the service standard to define the acceptable level of performance: "We answer 80% of queries within five days." The 80% is another operational figure, and most importantly, what happens to the 20% that miss the target? These are the kind of KPIs that have existed in organizations for years and still do. They are not completely useless, in that they allow the organization to do operational and resource planning. However, they are flawed in terms of delivering for customers. Most importantly, they normally have very little to do with true customer expectations since essentially they are internal metrics created for internal needs.

Another example of this type of measure is quality audit or monitoring. This is where an internal member of staff, normally a supervisor or manager, assesses the quality of work of another staff member. Again, completely sensible, but still seen from an internal perspective, even though they are considering what the customer would think of it.

This is not to say that internal metrics aren't useful, they are, but in terms of indicating customers' experiences or feelings, they have some limitations. They are very good for understanding the efficiency and effectiveness of a process, understanding resourcing requirements, and planning and understanding throughput. But to get a balanced view of performance for customers, they must be used in conjunction with other metrics. Used on their own, they could give an organization a completely false view of their performance for their customers. Calibration by customer requirements is essential.

2) Inside-Out Metrics

Some organizations realized the limitation of internal-only metrics and decided that an external perspective was required. Inside-out metrics are those that a 'customer' (chosen by the organization) experiences (a product or service) and reports back to the organization on the performance based on some agreed parameters or expectations. The most typical example of this is mystery shopping. The organization will often define for the mystery shoppers what they should look at and what standards that they would expect to see. This gives a different perspective to internal metrics, as it's a customer 'testing' the process from an external perspective. However, the customer is often guided by the organization. Another drawback is scale. In most circumstances, the amount of mystery shopping that can be carried out is limited and therefore may be seen as not completely representative of the service in that period. For example, if you send a mystery shopper into a store once a week, to test the experience, but that store serves 1,000 customers a week, is the mystery shop visit really representative? And even if you increased it to 10 mystery visits, would that be any different? But the reality is that mystery shopping is not meant to be statistically representative. It's almost testing the highest standard, and the random nature of it, which seemingly makes it unfair, is the thing that drives the highest standards of performance and makes it effective.

High standards drive service excellence and it is absolutely essential that an organization knows how it is performing against its own standards, and getting a customer to judge against these high standards is a great way to do it. This does not have to be a big formal system. It's amazing when I often ask senior managers at organizations, "Have you ever tried to ring your own contact centre or even use your own website?" Very few have. I'd always encourage anyone managing any part of a business to try and use their own business or team – it's amazing what you learn!

3) Outside-In metrics

Outside-in metrics are a fundamental part of understanding how the organization is performing for customers. It basically involves asking customers what they think in some scalable, systematic way, and getting customer feedback. What a novel idea! Clearly the idea of getting customer feedback has been around for some time, but it is in the last few years that it has become ubiquitous in most organizations.

Complaints First ...

The most basic form of customer feedback – that has been around since commerce began – is customer complaints. The beauty of complaints is that they are free feedback from customers who normally just want the organization to get better at what it does. Unfortunately, many organizations don't see it this way, and almost see complaints as customers 'moaning' and in many cases being unreasonable. This is a crazy mind-set to have. Customer complaints are almost the most important piece of information that an organization will get, along with sales figures. The most progressive organizations almost encourage complaints, as they are keen to understand if they are doing things wrong. There is the saying, "If you enjoyed our service, please tell your friends, and if you didn't, please tell us!" This takes on a completely different scale of importance in the social media age, but all organizations should have this attitude embedded in their culture. I call it having 'open ears'.

In my experience, the way an organization deals with its complaints tells you everything that you need to know about its culture toward customers. Organizations can be grouped into three broad and completely unscientific categories. First, you have the **avoiders**. These are organizations that spend most of the time trying to deny that complaints exist. They will log complaints but try and reclassify as many as possible as non-complaints. Also, they spend as much time arguing about the validity of complaints as dealing with them. Complaints are a 'slur' on the character of the business and something that is better swept under the carpet. Clearly they deal with complaints, but that's about it, and they certainly don't see them as a resource that can help improve the business. It's hard to believe that businesses like this exist, but they do. I've seen them!

Next are the **dealers**. These organizations are incredibly good at recognizing complaints, logging them in a system, and reporting on them. They are also very effective at dealing with complaints because they understand that a complainant dealt with well is very valuable. So they will often be very generous with any compensation or ex-gratia payments. However, they tend to 'spectate' the reasons that complaints exist, almost accepting that complaints will always exist and that the most important thing is that the customer is appropriately dealt with. This is not necessarily a bad thing. However, if you look at their data, they often get the same level of complaints about the same type of thing, year after year, and as long as this status quo is not changing too much, then little happens. I know these exist because I have managed complaints in this way previously. In this instance, the customer often goes away happy, but how healthy is it for the organization as a whole?

Lastly, we have the **eliminators**. Sounds awesome, right? These organizations do everything that a dealer does, but in addition, they are focused on the reason why complaints are occurring, in order to eliminate them. They not only log and analyse complaints, but they are obsessive about the root cause of the complaints. Once they understand the complaints, they put measures in place to improve what they are doing and reduce the number of complaints received. They look for effective and commercial ways to solve an issue and often involve their colleagues in finding the solutions. They are not afraid to try new ways of doing things because they are often already innovative businesses. *For an eliminator, there is no such things as a 'common complaint'. They fix these, fast.* Take Amazon. Bezos not only invites complaints by making his email address accessible, but he then has the whole question-mark thing. With this he is saying to his team not only what is this, or can you deal with this, but can we ensure that we find all cases like this and make sure we stop them occurring again. Amazon is a classic eliminator and understands that this is good for their customers and good for their business.

So complaints are an absolutely essential Outside-In metric, always have been and always will be. Organizations have to be realistic about which category they are in and strive to improve in order to be truly customer centred. If customers are really central to the purpose of the business, this shouldn't be too difficult. However, there is an issue with using complaints as your only customer feedback, in that complainants are clearly unhappy about something, but it doesn't mean that those that haven't complained are happy! There are three categories to consider:

1. Those who are just as unhappy as the complainers, but couldn't be bothered to complain and instead either moan incessantly or take their business elsewhere; let's call them the **'silent complainers'**.
2. Then there are those who aren't entirely happy but not unhappy enough to complain; let's call these **moderates**.
3. Customers who are generally happy, but see ways that the experience could be even better; let's call these **improvers**.

The problem is that if you just focus on complaints, the only way the issues of silent complainers will be addressed is that if they happen to be the same issues as the complainers. If their issues are different, you will not know. Likewise, you will not know the issues that moderates or improvers have. And the reality is that they often have different issues, not enough to cause them to complain, but all the same, an irritant that affects the overall experience. The only way to find out what moderates and improvers think is to ask them, and this gave birth to first customer satisfaction surveys and then all the other different methodologies for gathering customer feedback.

... Now Customer Feedback

At first, customer satisfaction surveys were great. Lots of different ways of asking customers what they think, from focus groups, to sending out questionnaires, to most recently post-call and online surveys. With time, technology has improved so that these can be carried out on scales that produce statistically significant results that can be split by organization, department, team, channel, product, and even individual. Surveys can be on almost any topic and the results analysed in real time. But regardless of this, the problem still persists. Conducting surveys alone does not make a customer-centred organization; rather, it is what the organization does about what they are hearing.

It is also important to know what to ask the customers. For many years, customers were asked about how satisfied they were with various things. Satisfied – you have to wonder how organizations would want to use such a weak word. Talk about being damned by faint praise! Satisfaction, almost by definition, means accept-able. "That meal was satisfactory" doesn't bring to mind a place that you would be in a hurry to try out! Most organizations asked it anyway and strived to be very or highly satisfactory, which sounds like an oxymoron! More importantly, lots of academic types proved that there was very little correlation between cus-tomers being satisfied and any of the major commercial metrics like loyalty or repurchase. That's not surprising, because being satisfied with something isn't really being emotionally connected to it, and it's the emotional connection that drives the loyalty and brand affinity. What made things worse is that most scores were averaged; a customer satisfaction score of 7.3 wasn't greatly useful. What most organizations began to do to further focus their per-formance was to look at the 'top box' scores; that means on a scale of 1-10, only the percentage of scores that are 9-10 are reported on. It is clear that moving that score is a lot more challenging and therefore more meaningful. So although organizations gathered information through millions of questionnaires, it was difficult to use the results and to connect them to commerciality.

Then in 2003, Fred Reicheld, a fellow at Bain and Company, wrote an article in the *Harvard Business Review* called, "One Number You Need to Grow" and followed it with his book, *The Ultimate Question*. In these he introduced the concept of the Net Promoter Score (NPS). (See *Figure 11*).

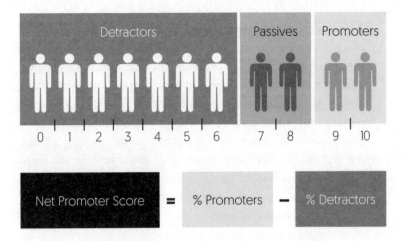

Figure 11: Net Promoter Score Methodology

The Net Promoter Score (NPS) identifies customers as detractors, neutrals, or promoters.

This works on the basis that you only need to ask customers one question: "How likely are you to recommend this product or service to family or friends?" Customers score the answer from 1 (low) to 10 (high). Depending on the score, customers are classified: detractors (1-6), neutrals (7-8), and promoters (9-10). The NPS is calculated by subtracting the percentage of detractors from the percentage of promoters. Almost overnight, NPS has become the most popular customer feedback metric. Why? First, it was claimed that there was a direct correlation between NPS and revenue growth. Also, the concept of recommendation is a strong emotional one because a customer would have to trust a product or an organization to recommend it to their loved ones. NPS suggests that it is just as important to convert detractors to neutrals, as it is to convert neutrals to advocates. Consequently, organizations know that they should focus as much on things that make customers unhappy as they do on those that make them happy. As an emotional metric, I believe that recommendation is a good proxy for trust and an easier question to ask customers.

There have been numerous papers attempting to discredit, if not the NPS measurement itself, certainly its alleged correlation to growth and revenue. It's at this point that I have to say that I don't really care! The first and most important thing is that companies are asking customers what they think. The common parlance for this is getting the 'Voice of the Customer' (VoC). What they ask customers is secondary to me, as long as they ask customers something meaningful, and they do it over a long enough period of time that they can do something about improving. It's about making them the focus of organizational activity and improving them.

One of the few drawbacks of customer feedback schemes is really a positive one in many ways. Often, there is almost always space for customers to say why they gave the scores they did, and suggest improvements. This makes perfect sense, as a score is a general marker of performance and something that can be improved on over time. But what needs improving? This can only come from analysing the verbatim comments. Remember, the silent complainers, moderates, and improvers. Well, customer feedback questionnaires are perfect for trying to understand their needs, and they will generally tell you. These comments will often be more valuable than the scores themselves.

Modern technology has come up with solutions for collating comments (word clouds and text and voice analytics) but none are yet particularly satisfactory for mining unstructured data such as this. Though, in my opinion, there is no substitute to grabbing a big sample of the comments and reading them yourself. It's amazing how themes emerge quickly and reading customers' actual words is very powerful, in a similar way to reading complaints. The same goes for customers' comments on social media. These are an incredibly valuable source of outside-in data, but very difficult to 'farm' effectively. The secret is to try to read as many as possible, because they tend to be live, 'in the moment' issues. Where possible they should be resolved as soon as possible. Being really good at this can be a brand differentiator.

The other benefit of feedback forms is all the positive comments people write. Lots of organizations fear asking customers for feedback because of the negative things that they will say. But in actual fact, customers write as many positive things as they do negative. These comments and stories can be incredibly powerful in motivating staff to continue to do a good job. When it's customers giving a 'well done' to staff it's even more special, and feedback forms of all types allow this opportunity. *The way to build a positive customer culture is to catch people doing the right thing and then celebrate it.*

4) **Outside-Out metrics**

Last but not least there are outside-out metrics. These are assessments of your performance made by customers, but not in relation to questions asked by your company. The most common example of this is industry benchmarking, where independent groups, often industry bodies, publications, or consultancies ask customers about a variety of companies and rank them in order of performance.

Why is this important for a balanced assessment of how an organization is performing for its customers? Well, in the competitive commercial world, service experience is an important differentiator, but in order for it to be an effective differentiator, it's important for an organization to know where it ranks relative to the opposition. Customer feedback normally only reveals an organization's own performance. So an organization could be 'patting itself on the back' for improving its service when its competitors have improved theirs too, and so they are still in the same position as far as customers were concerned. Additionally, an organization may be working to an SLA that is out of step with the rest of the industry ... only benchmarking would reveal that!

Customers also relate experience to the brand image of an organization, which can make benchmarking a bit confusing. For example, Aldi customers know that they will get their products at a cheaper price than they would at say Sainsbury's. As a result, they may have lower expectations of the service they receive, and are willing to put up with due to the price difference. If they receive better-than-expected service at the Aldi, when asked they may give Aldi a better score than Sainsbury's, not necessarily because the service was better in absolute terms, but relative to what their expectations were of both stores. This may seem a bit confusing, but hopefully it demonstrates how important it is for an organization to understand how customers rate its service experience relative to its competitors. This rating is just as important for an organization to understand as it is for it to know its price position.

Being able to benchmark your customer experience relative to a competitor is vital in today's fast moving and value driven environment.

So, What to Do with All This Data?

Most of the best customer-centric organizations will have a customer dashboard that will contain metrics from all the four quadrants of the matrix. This allows them to 'triangulate' and really understand their performance. But just as with complaints, this is not about collating data to show how clever an organization is. The key is what happens as a result. All customer data, regardless of how sparse it is, and regardless of what level it is collected at, should be the driver for 'the virtuous cycle of customer centricity'! (see *Figure 8* on page 125)

This is the simplest thing in the world, but incredibly powerful when embedded in the business.

It starts with listening to the voices of customers, to understand what's important to them, and then to monitor progress against these important 'customer get rights'. The next step is to understand what the customers are saying. There is a key difference between listening and understanding. Customers say a lot and they're often not totally clear about what they want, and it's not the job of customers to come up with solutions. This is often levelled as a criticism of customer feedback or VoC programme. Customers always know what they want and an organization just needs to understand what they are saying. If an organization understands what customers are saying and innovates around these, it won't go far wrong, especially around customer experience.

This brings us to the next step. Once an organization has listened to customers and understands what they want or need, then the key is to do something about it. Too many organizations have VoC programmes to listen to customers and then do very little with the output. But the key is to make a decision, hopefully to do something, but it doesn't always have to be. *Great service is not always about saying 'yes' to customers*. There can be many reasons why an organization or individual cannot do exactly what customers want, and many of these can be commercial. However, if customers have been listened to and understood, then perhaps an alternative solution that is also acceptable to customers can be found. It's important to be active around addressing customer needs, because if you are not, then someone else will be and customer experience is a competitive battlefield.

Lastly on the 'virtuous cycle' is 'tell'. After listening to customers, understanding what they want, doing something about it or maybe not, the organization must then let its customers know. This is a two-way relationship to establish. Common courtesy in a relationship is to let the customers know what has or hasn't been done. Otherwise customers may feel that their ideas and suggestions have fallen into a black hole. I'm not suggesting for a second that organizations should respond to every single comment, but a general way of communicating, "You said, we did" would be good for building customer relationships. But where possible, I do believe that if customers are invited to give feedback, it should always be acknowledged, and in this day and age that's not difficult.

Making Sure Something Happens

In order for the cycle of customer centricity to work, it must never stop. It just keeps on going: listening, understanding, acting, telling, and then listening again, on and on. This requires for the appropriate governance to be established. As the voice of the customers is being collated, it needs a group of people to understand what is being said and decide what action is going to be taken, and make sure that the actions are appropriately implemented. Many organizations have now established customer committees, whose role is to do just this. The higher up in the organization these groups are, the more chance there is of the required actions getting the attention needed to make them happen. For example, every month at Metro Bank, the executive leadership team spend half a day considering their VoC feedback and monitoring the various initiatives in place to improve the experience for customers. That is all they do at that meeting! That is another indicator to how customer centred an organization is. How much of the senior team's time is taken up considering how the organization is performing for its customers, not in terms of sales, but in terms of the customer experience? Someone very senior at an organization once said to me, "We have the ultimate measure of customer experience, it's called sales." Clearly, I don't agree with that! Customers might be buying a product due to lots of different factors, but it doesn't mean they like or feel that they have any sort of relationship with that organization. The danger here is that as soon as the product or price advantage is eroded, as they surely will be in today's fast changing world, customers will switch if they feel that their needs have been ignored. Just counting the money is no longer enough.

If we need to consider a great example of a comprehensive VoC programme, we need look no further than First Direct, the CX leader in the UK ... and remember, they're a bank! Originally a telephone bank, it is this that they are still famous for. So they focus on 'post-call' surveys to which they get an unprecedented response rate, something in the region of 68%, which suggests that their customers are keen and happy to talk to them. They use these surveys to continuously look for things that they can improve. This along with post-purchase surveys, complaints analysis, agent feedback, social media listening, and speech analytics goes into a 'melting pot' to create the Voice of the Customer Dashboard, which is reviewed at the VoC Forum that meets monthly and is chaired by the CEO, Tracy Garrard. At this group, not only do they review the performance of the organization through the customers' eyes, but they also review in detail the top five improvement initiatives in detail, as well as understanding what the next five are! Tracy is always quick to point out that this forum is not one of her smart ideas. It has been there since day one, just a part of the way they do things at First Direct. Although one of the things that she must take credit for is 'Tracy's Island'. This is both a series of forums and message boards that allow colleagues to let Tracy know directly what things need to happen to continue to improve things for the customers, therefore keeping everyone in the loop.

It's not only the senior teams that need to understand how the organization is performing for customers – it's also everyone else. Once an initial direction has been communicated to colleagues, through the vision and purpose, it's really important to give them regular updates on progress as well as allow opportunities to be engaged in any improvement activity. It's incredible how effective communication of a target and progress can create incredible momentum and changes of behaviour. This is especially the case if any targets are linked to some sort of bonus. Most major organizations have created some sort of reward structure and linked it to achievement of targets relating to the customer performance metrics. Such is the growing importance of bonuses for customer metrics that it is now only secondary to bonuses for revenue. In fact, in many organizations, customer-facing staff members are only given bonuses on customer metrics, as this is what they can influence most directly.

Creating a reward scheme based on customer metrics should be approached with extreme caution. They always sound like such a good idea – 'do a better job for customers, and you earn more money'. Everyone wins, right? But sometimes bonus schemes can be governed by 'the law of unintended consequences' … where something created for all the right reasons produces the wrong behaviours! Any time that rewards, especially monetary ones, are introduced, some people try and 'game the system' by trying to find easy ways to earn the money. This can be an issue with individuals within a team who are trying to achieve their bonus.

Often the managers are as much of a problem as the front line. They may ask colleagues to focus only on the areas that are being measured by the metrics, and ignore everything else, so there will be areas of the customer experience that will be neglected because they're not covered in the metrics.

This shows the power of being very clear about what's important to customers and being very transparent about how it will be measured and linked to reward. Pret a Manager are a great example of how to get this whole reward thing right. I'm a very loyal customer and have always marvelled at their incredible levels of service and the energy of all their staff, regardless of where you visit their stores. I'll be honest, I've been envious at times. Since having the opportunity to study them in more detail, there are many reasons they are so good. The reward scheme at Pret a Manager is a thing of beauty, and I believe has a significant impact on their service. They use an extensive mystery-shopping programme, which is very simple. At Pret a Manager they have six key points of service, their 'fundamental truths': presentation, selection, queue speed, table cleanliness, and 'thank you'.

They have 10 questions for the mystery shopper that relate to these points of service, and the mystery shopper ranks performance from 1-5. They have high standards, and a score of 3-5 on every question earns the whole store a bonus ... and the bonus is very generous, a significant uplift in their salary! They also have a cash award for an individual colleague who provides outstanding service. In addition, the top 10% of stores receives £25 per head to spend on a team event every month, as long as they have achieved bonuses every week and have at least one outstanding individual colleague visit. This is already great, but the clever bit is that it links behaviours and outcomes that are important for the organization with the organization's required standards. You only get the bonus if you have not been late or sick. The 'cherry on top of the cake' for me is that the bonus is paid on a weekly basis, so performance is linked to almost instant reward. If you don't make it one week, you can have another go next week! This is absolutely vital. In addition, this scheme is totally integrated into the DNA of the organization and when new staff members are being trained they are told what is important to customers, how their behaviours and actions can influence that, and if they achieve this, how they can expect to benefit. Good for the customer, good for the staff, and good for the company. This scheme costs them a significant amount of money compared to their overall turnover, but that doesn't deter them, and they have apparently never worked out the Internal Rate of Return (IRR) on the programme. It's just part of what makes Pret, Pret! Everybody 'gets it' and buys into the programme from the start. This creates a strong and focused work ethic, with everyone pulling together. I think it's a work of genius!

How It Worked at Sainsbury's

When I joined Sainsbury's, they had the building blocks of a very comprehensive customer dashboard. First, they were very clear on the fundamental truths of retailing from a service experience perspective. This is because when Justin King set off on his mission to Make Sainsbury's Great Again (MSGA), he had to re-establish what the customers fundamentally wanted from a supermarket: availability, pleasant environment, good people interaction, and easy to get out. Knowing how important these were, he created two absolutely iconic mystery-shopping programmes to ensure that the whole organization would be focused on delivering the right things for customers.

The first of these was called Making Availability Count (MAC). On a weekly basis, every shop in the country would receive a mystery shopper, who would look for 50 prearranged items. The store would lose points for every item that couldn't be found. This was a test for the logistics of the whole organization and ensured that everyone had a common goal of getting it right. Perhaps it was not an entirely fair system to all staff at all times but it did reinforce the importance of ensuring that products were available for customers when then they needed them. Empty shelves are the enemy, and if it took 50,000 mystery shops a year for people to get that, then so be it. Good customer metrics do that: they make sure all staff know the importance of that customer need and set exceptionally high standards of delivery, especially for the things that are important to customers.

The second mystery-shopping programme was called Making Customers Matter (MCM). This tested the standards of the shop in terms of cleanliness of the store and availability of things like baskets, how colleagues were interacting with customers, and how quickly a customer could get out of the shop, i.e., the length of queues. These visits took place every two weeks and were a significant focus for all colleagues.

Both of these were very important and reflected significantly upon bonuses received; hence the fairness of the programmes frequently came into question. How could a visit by one mystery shopper for less than an hour, interacting with a couple of colleagues, be a fair representation of a store's work? Particularly as most stores employ around 300 – 400 staff, serve around 30,000 customers in a two-week period, and are open for almost 100 hours per week.

It may not be fair, but it's right! Every store is being tested against the same standards and these standards are things that are fundamentally important to customers, so they are not things that were expected some of the time, they were expected all of the time. So really, it didn't matter if it was the first, fiftieth, or 15,000th customer, the same high standards needed to be met. When you think about it, that's actually being fair to customers. Could a store get unlucky? Yes, they could, but these things tended to equal themselves out over the course of a year. The best stores just made sure they were 'on point' every minute of the day, and that way, they would 'win' more than they would 'lose', but more importantly, the customers would gain all of the time. I believe an incentive scheme only works when the behaviour that it drives is good for the customers, and this is where you need to always be conscious of the 'law of unintended consequences'.

Retail is incredibly competitive and it is imperative to understand how you are doing against the competition so that you can crawl 'one inch farther'. The great thing about benchmarking service experience is that the benchmarking company just has to go out and ask a bunch of customers questions or send a group of mystery shoppers into a shop! For a major brand like Sainsbury's, this happens all the time and there are lots of service league tables that such an organization may end up on that have nothing to do with them directly! I suppose the secret is to ignore the ones with the poor results and to celebrate the ones with good results, which is what many organizations do. There is always a way to argue with the methodology, the sample size, or the analysis, but this may be a mistake. External benchmarking can be quite valuable and something to learn from, especially when it doesn't seem to agree with your internal data. Are your customers telling you something you don't already know? Also, your relative position is really important too. Are others performing better than you, and if so, is there something you can learn from them?

So hopefully, it's clear that some sort of balanced customer scorecard is vital to understanding how well the organization is performing for its customers. I have not experienced a first-class customer-centric organization that doesn't have this and doesn't use it to drive focus on customers and the right culture in the business. It doesn't have to be grand and complicated, but it does have to be transparent, make sense, and drive the right behaviours in the organization, and outcomes for the customers. I am often asked whether one measure is more important or relevant than another. My belief is that they all tell a slightly different story, and I think that getting as many different perspectives is important, relative to the budget that is available. For example, getting the customers' view is vital and I would always encourage it. But given that all customers have different views and different standards, it is also important to set high standards for what customers need or want, and to measure it through a mystery shop. A lot of the high performing organizations do this, as it allows them to set a standard, higher than the customers' expectations, which means they have more chance of achieving it consistently … straight customer feedback doesn't always give you that.

CHAPTER SEVEN

It Starts and Ends with Leadership

A few weeks ago, I heard a couple of ladies having a chat about work. One said to the other, "So how's work, then?"

The other said, "You know, same old crap, day after day, still, you've got to pay the bills somehow!"

As a leader, it's this sort of statement that makes my heart sink. This lady was clearly not very engaged in her work and was just going there to pick up her weekly pay. In many ways, there's nothing wrong with that; it's just a missed opportunity. Imagine the impact of her attitude if she spends all her time dealing with customers, either internal or external? I don't see this as a failure of the individual, I see it as a failure of the leadership within that organization. This may appear harsh, but I believe that in great service organizations, it begins and ends with effective leadership.

Leadership is probably the most written-about discipline in most professional fields, whether it's business, politics, or sport. And with good reason: it is the thing that drives achievement, and everyone wants to know how to be a great leader. When it comes to creating service excellence, it is no less important, although it is multi-faceted. The organization needs to have a strong sense of vision and purpose, and to be about putting the customer at the heart of the business. This needs to be as evident in their actions as well as in their words, and it must start at the top of the organization. Every high-perform-ing, customer-centred business has this: a CEO or MD who always speaks about how important customers are to the organization. They specify a clear vision and establish a set of values so that everyone is focused on the customer. Just as in a cult, they set the tone.

Is that alone enough? I don't think it is. I have had a few conversa-tions with leaders who really do believe in being customer centric and it making a difference to the business. They act in the right way and say all the right things, but it doesn't seem to make a difference; customers don't love the business and they struggle to make any improvements in the customer metrics that they hold dear. They say to me, "What more can I do? I keep telling everybody who will listen how important this is to me and the whole organization!"

Leadership – Top, Middle, and Bottom!

There is a Peter Drucker quote that I love: "Culture eats strategy for breakfast." And probably for lunch and dinner, too. Senior leaders can shout platitudes until they are blue in the face; however, unless middle management believes in it and has the capability to deliver it, there is no chance that it will result in action at the front line. This is a concept that I like to call, *'middle management glue'*. Basically the message gets stuck somewhere down the pipe. Some senior leaders recognize it and instead of cascading the message down the management chain, they try to engage the front-line staff directly. This works for a period of time, but if middle-management glue is part of the culture, it will kill that, too. If middle management glue is part of the culture, the solution is quite simple: change the managers or, change the managers!

This makes middle-managers sound like cynical and manipulative people, and most of them are not. The reality is that middle management is a difficult place to be. It is their role to convert strategy that is coming down the line into something that makes operational sense for front-line colleagues who are not necessarily that interested in it. That's pretty tough to do. At the same time, the same senior managers are tasking them with getting the operation running efficiently and effectively and doing it on a budget that is normally being unreasonably squeezed. They have metrics and KPIs and audits and operational challenges and sickness and grievances and restructures coming out of their ears! The last thing they need to hear is the new CEO's customer-centric strategy. As I said, it's a tough place to live.

What's worse is that many aren't clear on what's expected of them, and even if they are, nobody has really told them how they are supposed to deliver it. At its core is a lack of education – not really academic, more leadership skills and capabilities. It's a bit like becoming a parent…bear with me on this one. Nothing really prepares anyone for becoming a parent. How many people actually learn how to be a good parent by going on a course, reading articles, and studying? I suspect very few.

The same can be said for managers and leaders. Most get promoted for being good in one particular role, and suddenly they have responsibility for a bunch of other people and they are told to get on with it! Most organizations do not take enough time and trouble to make their managers ready to be leaders and this has enormous implications. It contributes significantly to the whole management glue situation, as some of the managers struggle to understand and interpret the vision and values coming down from the senior leaders. More importantly, they struggle to get the best out of the people who work for them. "Same old crap, day after day" is a direct consequence of that. Life, business, and service excellence are all about people. If an organization is having a problem with achieving service excellence, the first place to look is not the people delivering the service, but the people leading them. Most of us know the phrase, "People join companies, but they leave managers." It's that important.

How Should Service Leaders Make People Feel

If we agree that people are the most important resources to a business, then how do we want our people to 'feel'? Usually the answer is that we want employees to be engaged. But I like to think about it slightly differently. I think employees need to have three attributes, which I like to call the Employee Trinity: engagement, alignment, and empowerment (see *Figure 12* over the page).

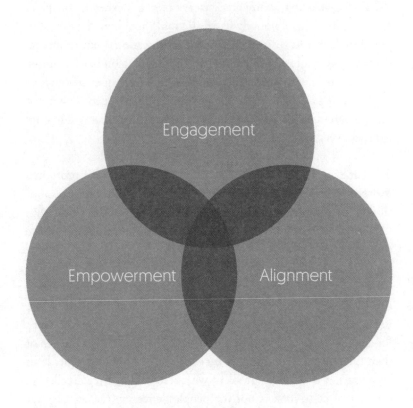

Figure 12: The 'Perfect' Employee Trinity

The Employee Trinity includes engagement, alignment,
and empowerment.

- Engagement – employees like working here, it's a good place to work, and they feel happy
- Alignment – employees know how what they do on a daily basis makes a difference to the organization as a whole, whether it's answering calls, producing spreadsheets, or cleaning floors. They need to understand how their small cog helps to turn the 'big' wheel. They need to understand 'why'? One of my favourite quotes is *"Give a man a why, and he'll conquer any 'how'."*

- Empowerment – the employees' ability to make decisions that make a difference for customers, to make things happen. This is all about colleagues being confident that they have the 'permission' to act and the freedom to 'get it wrong, but for the right reasons' … the right reason being, trying to help customers.

If all staff members exhibit the employee trinity – they are happy to be there, they are connected to the goals of the organization, and they feel what they do makes a difference both for the organization as a whole and for their customers – that would be an amazing place to work. All three of these elements are very related, but the 'sweet spot' is where all three exist.

So how do we make this happen? Well, one type of organization for whom this is easier is small business. Certainly they find alignment much clearer, they are normally fun places to work where everyone knows each other and what they do, and also people usually have a very specific task or tasks that they are empowered to do, mainly because there is no one else around to do it. The problems come as an organization grows and more and more layers of management are introduced, creating more distance between the messages from the top of the organization and the execution at the bottom. And in these layers of managers, we don't necessarily have the individuals with the ability to convert vision into action as we have described. So it would be good – certainly in this instance – to think like a big business and behave like a small one.

People often talk about how important it is to get the culture of a business right if you want employees to behave in the way that you want them to. This is undoubtedly true and why there is so much written about culture being 'the way that we do things around here'. As a result, there is often talk about culture change programmes, but it is impossible to influence or create a culture directly. *Culture is something that grows out of an environment that is created*. Then, creating the right environment ensures that the right culture can flourish. The biggest determinant of the environment is leadership at all levels, but particularly in middle management. These are the people who really define 'the way we do things around here'. They control the environment, so they create the culture and drive behaviour. They are the people who make things 'real' for the colleagues that work for them. Yet, they are often the least invested in population! (see *Figure 13*)

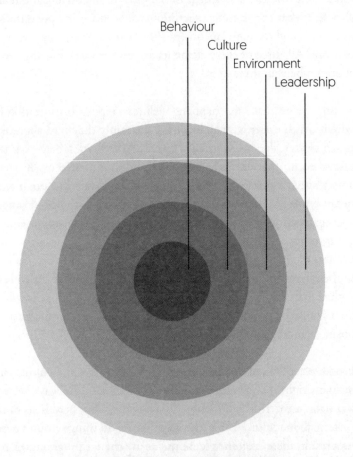

Figure 13: How Leadership Drives Behaviour

Middle management may be the biggest determinant of an organization's culture and environment.

What Do Good Service Leaders Look Like?

I believed for some time that the key to service excellence was leadership – difficult to prove empirically, but very easy to do so anecdotally. One of the reasons I joined Sainsbury's was that I would get the opportunity to 'study' leadership at all levels and the difference that it made to the performance of colleagues, and do it at a reasonable scale. However, there was one set of observations that really made the whole concept of the importance of leadership come to life. As a senior director at Sainsbury's, I was invited to the annual long-service awards dinner for colleagues who had been with the organization for more than 25 years. At these events, I got to talk to people who had really seen the business evolve, and I would always ask the same questions. "In your time at Sainsbury's, you must have worked for lots of managers." The answer was obviously yes, and the number varied from between 10 to 20. I'd then ask them to remember the best one and asked them to tell me what made that manager good. They always remembered good managers for the impact that they had had. What was most interesting were the reasons why they were so good, and I can assure you that the answers were always – without fail – the same or at least very similar:

- He was friendly and he always said hello
- He was like one of us
- He knew our names and the names of my family members
- He was always around and always helped out
- He always let us know what was going on
- When we did well, he'd take us down the pub or buy us cakes
- Customers always knew who he was and liked him, too

I would also ask about the managers that they didn't like, and the answer would unsurprisingly be the very opposite. We can get the picture pretty quickly, as we've all either had bad managers or heard of them. What was also interesting was that most of these 'bad' managers usually came to a rather unfortunate end in their professional lives. So if the answer is so easy, then why don't we have more great leaders in middle management? That was the next question that my team and I set out to answer.

To get an idea which were the high-performing stores we used customer service feedback scores, mystery shopping scores, and employee engagement scores. I visited the high performing stores up and down the country and met with managers and colleagues to find out what they did to make themselves so successful, even though I already had an idea: it was simply good leadership.

So This Is Service Leadership!

After months of analysis and research, I created service leadership. It was based on everything that I had experienced over my whole career, but particularly what I had seen in the retail environment. This is leadership with a specific objective of getting the best out of colleagues in order to provide excellent service to customers. This is the point of service leadership: it is not some nebulous leadership methodology, it had to be practical and easy to grasp, almost as if staff had always known it, but had forgotten how to apply some of the principles.

Service leadership is based on four pillars: visibility, inspiration, accountability, and customer proximity (see *Figure 14*).

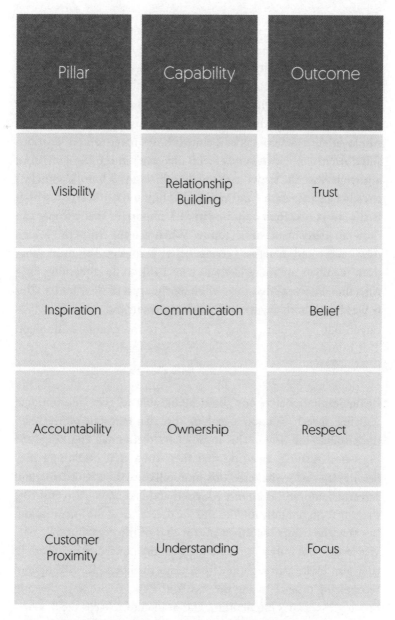

Pillar	Capability	Outcome
Visibility	Relationship Building	Trust
Inspiration	Communication	Belief
Accountability	Ownership	Respect
Customer Proximity	Understanding	Focus

Figure 14: The Service Leadership™ model at a glance

The four pillars of service leadership include visibility, inspiration, accountability, and customer proximity.

Visibility

The concept of visibility is about always being around for your team. Yes, it's about being seen, but also being available, rather than always on the way to a meeting. When leaders are available, they can build relationships with members of the team and the team as a whole, which in turn fosters better teamwork and peer-to-peer relationships. Any team with a family feel is one that is more engaging to be a part of. Also, the leader needs to be able to give a bit of themselves to create a transparency and approachability and **build trust, which is the most precious commodity**. It's important that a leader can show an element of vulnerability. When a team trusts the leader, they believe and therefore become better followers. This means that team members are more likely to take a risk to do something for a customer, knowing that they will have the trust of their leader. This is the core to both engagement and empowerment.

Inspiration

Being inspirational is not about being able to give an emotional 'rallying' speech, but about making sure that everyone on the team understands the 'why'. This means how their small cog keeps the big wheel turning, ensuring that they know that everything they do – every day – matters. This requires constant enthusiastic and positive communication of both good and bad news. Also ensuring that the team not only understand the objectives of the organization, but that the team's objectives mirror that of the organization's. Service leaders not only paint a picture with their own communication, they also invite participation from team members. Rewarding and recognizing progress along the way to the goal is also key; cheering on progress creates momentum, and momentum keeps the flywheel turning. Inspiration is the core of engagement and alignment.

Accountability

Accountability is a core belief for all service leaders; they understand that, although they need to be accountable for the performance of the team, ownership needs to be taken within the team. Accountable leaders actually 'give control rather than taking control', as David Marquet wrote in his excellent book, *Turn the Ship Around*. This means that effective delegation needs to be a key skill, building on trust and allowing team members to do their thing, while never abdicating responsibility. I once had a conversation with a store manager whose customer metrics were terrible. When I pointed this out to him, he agreed and promptly told me how bad his customer service manager was and how he was hoping to replace him shortly. When I asked, "What about you?" his answer was, "What about me?"

In order to be clear about accountability, it is important to set goals and manage performance, both recognizing and praising positive performance and, almost more importantly, dealing promptly and fairly with underperformance. When it is not addressed, poor performance is like a cancer for service leadership. It erodes trust, respect, teamwork and performance, and undermines all relationships. A safe environment needs to be created for people to learn and take risks, and make mistakes as part of that process. This is how individuals and teams improve, and they can only do that if they know that they have permission, and that their leader will take accountability for any mistakes.

This is fundamental to creating empowerment and engagement.

Customer Proximity

Know whom *your* customers are and understand what makes them happy and sad. This is the pillar that is particularly focused on service excellence. This is just as valid for internal customers as it is for external ones. Once service leaders understand what their customers want, they create tangible measures to understand the team's performance.

My favourite example of creatively measuring performance is from a restaurant manager who wanted to know if meals were delivered to customers quickly enough. He placed a cup with one red and one green counter on each table, and asked customers to decide whether they had waited an acceptable time or not. All they had to do is put a green counter in the cup if they were happy with the time, and a red one if they weren't. Very simple, very visual, and very effective. He shared this with the whole restaurant team, both front of house and in the kitchen: no red counters today! Once they had the feedback, the team could work on improvements together, both what they have done well, and what they needed to improve. Everyone is on the journey. This is another attribute of a good service leader: the ability to get the whole team involved in 'closing the loop' on customer feedback – what they need to do to improve and being relentless about doing so.

Innovation is as much about the million small things that make a difference to customers as it is about the next big thing. This is where great leaders can make a difference by creating the environment where ideas will grow and flourish. This is truly inspirational.

The key output of service leaders is the environment that they create for their team in which to operate. When we think about it practically, they create a 'mood' for the team and that comes as much from their personal moods. Great leaders create the 'mood music' for their teams and enable great colleagues to shine – to feel engaged, aligned, and empowered to do their jobs without fear. Great teams are a reflection of their leaders; however, great leaders are continually 'looking in the mirror' to reflect on how they're performing and what they can do better.

The success of a service leadership programme is not only through courses such as communication, coaching, or problem solving. It's also how the pillars and the capabilities that support them are embedded in the performance. Unless they are assessed against these capabilities, very little progress will be made. At the end of the day, these are just more words unless they are turned into actions and behaviours that will benefit the organization as a whole. And to do this, it has to start from the top down. It's imperative that leadership capabilities form the backbone of every performance conversation for every leader in the business – otherwise the initiative will fail.

On the back of performance conversations there needs to be consequences for not behaving in the way that the organization desires. It's so easy to gloss over this; however, this doesn't happen at the best organizations. They have a near zero tolerance for the wrong sort of behaviours, even if they are producing the right sort of results. If you want to have a high performing culture, you cannot afford to carry any behavioural passengers. Everyone needs to buy into the behaviours and adhere to it – like they do in a cult. This is not about creating 'robots' and ignoring diversity. It's really important to build relationships with your team – 'the what' in order to build in trust 'the why'. This is a blueprint, a framework, to be a great service leader.

Originally when we rolled this out at Sainsbury's, we thought we might use the two-day training session as an assessment centre to weed out the managers that wouldn't be able to meet expectations. However, this didn't seem fair; many of the leaders only really knew how to manage as they had been managed, so it seemed unfair to penalize them for that. Instead, it made more sense to show them the light, hardwire the behaviours into the performance conversations and see where we got to from there. People are generally taught how to be managers rather than how to be leaders. It is widely accepted that these are two different things. Both are important to a high performing organization, but the more senior you are in an organization, the more leadership behaviours need to be exhibited (see *Figure 15*).

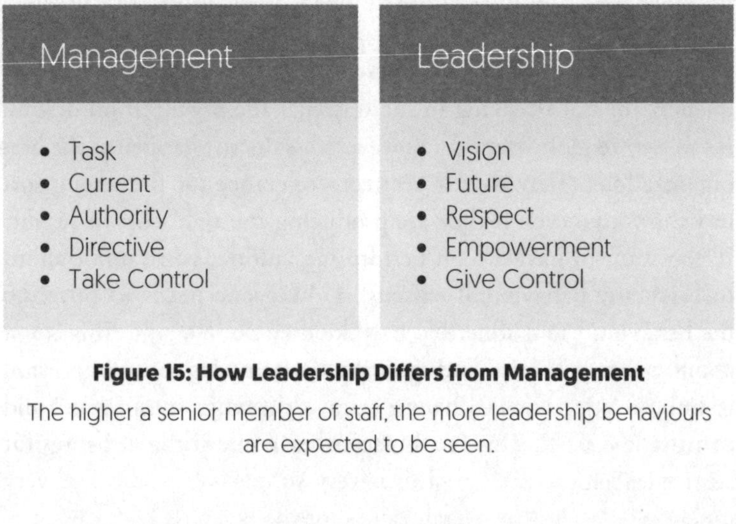

Management	Leadership
• Task	• Vision
• Current	• Future
• Authority	• Respect
• Directive	• Empowerment
• Take Control	• Give Control

Figure 15: How Leadership Differs from Management
The higher a senior member of staff, the more leadership behaviours
are expected to be seen.

Management is very much based in the here and now, concerned with tasks that need to be completed, and it is very effective when there are defined tasks to be done in a pressing timeframe. Managers get people to do things by exercising their authority" "Do this because I've told you to do it and I'm the boss." For that reason, managers are very directive.

Leadership is, as we have discussed, more about creating a vision of what the team is trying to achieve and making everything that the team does every day fit into that. It's about the future, more than it is about the present and everyone understanding how they fit into building the future. Leaders get things done through respect and building trust, and tend to ask people to do something rather than tell them to do it. Leaders empower their teams to come up with solutions and finding ways of getting things done. It's easy to see how these capabilities would exist more in senior management groups, but the big win is to have leaders throughout the whole organization, at all levels.

Clearly all the great organizations get this. If we think back to the cult that is Metro Bank, not only do they have AMAZE, which everyone in the organization adheres to, but in order to reinforce this for their management, they created AMAZE-ING – ING being the management behaviours that they looked for. The I is for Inspire, the N is for Nurture – getting the best out of people through – and last, the G is for Game-Changer – not accepting the status quo and consistently looking for areas where they could improve things for customers and colleagues. This is very simple, very clear, and very much in line with the overall values for the business.

I'd also always been really impressed by the role that leadership had played in the transformation of Boots the Chemist. When I spoke to Simon Roberts, the CEO, about it, one other key area that he spoke about is really understanding the customer. For him that was really important, but there was an issue in that 80% of the Boots customers were female, yet 80% of their store management population was male. In order to ensure that they could establish that empathy and certainly establish more customer proximity, Simon began a process to redress that imbalance. At the same time, he was focused on getting a great store manager in every store. In order to do that he had to think differently about the way the leaders in the organization would be. He thinks of leaders as having three perspectives on which they should be assessed: a performance leader, a change leader, and inspiring others. This is very much in line with what they have achieved at Metro Bank and in line with the whole concept of service leadership, and has been one of the factors driving the continued improvement in service performance over the last few years.

I once heard Sir David Brailsford, the successful British cycling coach, talk about outperformance and leadership, when he said, **"If you're a leader, you're an educator,"** and I think in saying that he hit the 'nail on the head'. Service leadership is about educating your team. Educating them in what they are there to achieve, and what it means. Educating them on how to work well together, about the standards that they need to achieve to consistently meet customer needs, and the progress that they are making toward it. Educating them that they can make a difference for customers and colleagues. Do this and I guarantee you will build an incredible environment in your team and over time the culture will grow out of this, because it will just be 'the way we do things around here'. This is more powerful than any operating model or strategy, which is back to where we started: get the right culture and let it do the 'heavy lifting'.

CHAPTER EIGHT

It's People that Make the Magic Happen

The worst-kept secret in driving service excellence is that it is the people that make the difference – the employees and colleagues working in an organization – whether they are directly serving customers or not. Yet, it is incredible how many organizations forget this in their quest to improve things for customers. Most start by focusing on measurement, systems and processes. These are all very important, but mean very little without having the right people around to make it all work. I love the quote from the great man himself, Walt Disney:

> *"You can design and create and build the most wonderful place in the world. But it takes people to make the dream a reality"*

Don't Train Service Excellence – Recruit It!

People who are going to be good with customers are most likely born and not made. These people have attributes that are very difficult to teach; however, some people have the right attributes, and they just haven't had them sparked by the right environment and culture. Therefore, the level of excellence that an organization can achieve can be defined by two incredibly significant disciplines: **recruitment, to ensure that it gets the right people, and performance management, to ensure that it recognizes the good ones and weeds out the bad ones.**

Note: I did not say training. I have very mixed views about customer service training, per se, and have rarely instigated it at any organization that I have worked for or with. As I've alluded to, I believe that if you sort out your leadership, recruitment, and performance management, you will be 90% of the way there. I think people fall into three categories: the people who can do it, those who can't do it, and ones that can do it but don't. The people that can don't need the training, as they already 'get it'. The people that can't do it don't need the training, because it won't make any difference – they can't do it! And the people who can but don't may be reminded by the training, but the only thing that will make them do it is the right environment, leadership, incentivization, recognition, and performance management. They know what they need to do, they just need to be encouraged to do it consistently. So it might be harsh to say that customer-service training is completely pointless, but in my opinion, there are numerous other things that should be above it on the shopping list!

'Recruit for attitude, train for skill' is possibly one of the most hackneyed terms in all of business, but that is because it is completely correct. The most important step is to **understand what a great colleague looks like for your particular organization**. If an organization is going to be like a cult, there must be attributes that define what great followers looks like. Every organization has employees that it defines as excellent. Find out what they are made of! The key to creating a cult of service excellence is to find as many people as possible that are made of the 'right stuff' and have the right attributes. At Sainsburys, we asked thousands of customers and colleagues what the right attributes were to deliver great service. They came up with five words: friendly, helpful, enthusiastic, genuine, and knowledgeable. You could argue that the only one of these that was trainable was knowledgeable. So finding and keeping the right people is imperative. We talked earlier about the mood that is created by the leader. This is very important since it will encourage the desired attributes to surface. *The wrong mood created by the wrong leader can make even the most enthusiastic and happy person miserable.*

So there is evidence that shows that at the heart of great service organizations there is an understanding of what colleagues' attributes should be. At Disney, they talked about happiness as a key attribute for employees. This makes perfect sense with their own mission, which is to make customers happy. This isn't happy as a passing mood, it is happiness as a state of mind … this person is a 'happy person'. Again, this isn't trainable, it exists in people. The better the environment they work in, the more likely it is to show itself on a consistent basis. In his book, *Happy Hour is 9-5*, Alexander Kjerulf, chief happiness officer at his company, WooHoo Inc., talks about the importance of being happy at work. Alexander is Danish, and it's a well-known fact that Danish people are very happy in general. The key here is that organizations that have happy employees outperform those that don't. So to have excellent customer service, happy people must be employed – sounds like a statement of the obvious to me!

Be clear on the Required Behaviours

Another organization that is legendary for its customer service in the United States is Southwest Airlines. Much has been written about how they achieve such excellence and, of course, it is multi-faceted. However, I have always been struck by their focus on getting people with the right attitude. They look for three attributes:

- A warrior spirit – that is, a desire to excel, act with courage, persevere, and innovate
- A servant's heart – the ability to put people first, treat everyone with respect, and proactively serve customers
- A fun-loving attitude – passion, joy, and aversion to taking oneself too seriously!

How fabulous are these, such evocative and emotional statements of what it takes to be an employee of South West? You would know when you were working in an organization where everyone had these attributes, and more importantly, you would know if you were a customer of an organization like this. I particularly love the 'servant's heart' attribute. One of the fundamental things about getting the right people with a service mind-set is that they are prepared to serve – that's what service is. This does not make the individuals 'servants', but it is a mind-set that many people struggle with. I think this is also a cultural problem: people in the East are more comfortable with this than say, northern Europeans. It is no surprise that airlines like Etihad and Emirates are legendary for the way that their employees provide service to their customers...meeting their every need, but with pride and dignity.

At Pret A Manger, they have built their business around being crystal clear what it takes to be one of their employees. They look for:

- Passion – not necessarily a passion for sandwiches or for customers, but a passion for 'something', the ability to be emotional about something
- Clear talking – this is about being genuinely empathetic and talking honestly on a peer-to-peer basis
- Teamwork – it's essential to be able to function as a member of a team and understand that success is all about one team delivering together.

They are famous for saying that "It's easy to train anyone in how to make sandwiches, but do they have the right behaviours?" Anyone who is a customer of Pret would agree that it is easy to understand that these are the behaviours that they look for in a Pret employee, as you can see and feel them every day when you are in one of their stores! They have a very simple saying: "Happy Team, Happy Customers, Happy Pret!" It's as simple as that!

So understanding how you want your employees to be, the desired attributes they should have, is imperative. Organizations should be crystal clear on this, as it supports the whole cultural framework of the organization that drives good customer service. These attributes or behaviours set an expectation for everyone in the organization as to how they will have to behave personally to work there.

Embed the Behaviours in the Colleague Lifecycle

Once an organization is clear on what it takes to work there, then what? Well, this is the essential acid test of how customer-centric an organization is. How hard wired are the attributes and behaviours into the employee lifecycle of the organization? (See *Figure 16*).

Figure 16: The HR Disciplines to Embed Employee Expectation Into

The more employees embrace the attributes and behaviours of an organization, the longer the employee lifecycle.

Every employee goes through this lifecycle – wherever they work, everywhere in the world. It effectively defines an organization, and most of it is in the remit of the human resources function, which normally sets the standards for how the employee lifecycle operates. If this is right, then the right environment will be created to give the best chance of achieving service excellence.

My former boss at Sainsburys, Gwyn Burr, always talked about *'colleagues being the last five yards to the customer'*. So it was important to invest in them. What she meant is that the company could invest millions of pounds in creating a store and filling it with product, but it was often the interaction with a colleague that could really make the difference. The organization had understood the importance of having customer experience and colleagues so closely aligned.

To make a difference in an organization, the culture of the business has to be shifted by influencing every single colleague, and it is essential to have the help of the people to do that. Let's consider each element of the employee lifecycle in turn.

1) **Recruitment Branding**

   Most people think about branding as part of the marketing mix and what organizations do to sell products and services to customers, and that many organizations spend vast amounts of money developing, maintaining, and protecting their brands. However, there is another side of an organization's brand, and that is what it tells its prospective employees. It's important to establish with potential employees what will be expected of them even before they look at a job description. The recruitment brand should make it clear "What it's like to work here" and "How we expect you to be." This should be clear on everything that a candidate may see – especially the website, as this is where most people go to find out about working at the organization.

   Aldi describes what is expected of prospective employees on its website, and that is to 'work hard', among other things. They don't use those words exactly, but phrases like, 'you'll be a grafter', 'you'll need bags of energy', and 'no standing around'. These make it abundantly clear in advance of any application what to expect if you end up working there. I realized that at

Sainsbury's we had to make sure that our recruitment brand reflected our required behaviours, not only to ensure that we recruited friendly people, but also to ensure that, later down the line, when they are asked to be friendly, or reprimanded for not being friendly, it wouldn't come as a big surprise. As a result, we changed all the website materials on the career pages to ensure that the wording reflected what would be required from new colleagues.

It's imperative to set out your stall from the earliest opportunity.

2) Assessment and Recruitment

Recruitment is one of the most important disciplines that any organization undertakes, especially with regard to service excellence. There is much made of the 'War for Talent' in the business press, but this is normally in reference to the most senior management and technical roles. However, the same applies to customer-facing roles. Organizations are only as good as the people that are dealing with their customers, and therefore, it's key to put significant time and trouble into getting it right. How often do you hear a manager say to her 'star' employee, "If only I had 'x' many more like you!" *It's important to try and make every hire one that makes your organization better.*

The first thing is to be clear about what behaviours are required and not wavering from it, under any circumstances. During the recruitment process at Sainsbury's, we realized that the online assessment questions being used had little to do with the five capabilities that we were looking for. So we engaged an occupational psychologist to change the questions and required answers to ensure that the right sort of people made it through. Following that, we had reports of the increase in capability of the individuals who were coming forward for interviews.

The next challenge was to ensure that the recruiters – normally the managers – had zero tolerance for candidates that didn't meet the behavioural requirements. Although this sounds simple in principle, it was often hard to do in practice. Many managers were under significant operational pressures and by the time they met candidates, they were desperate to recruit people to help get things done in the store. It's at this point that it's tempting to stop thinking of the candidates as vital cogs in the service experience 'wheel', and just 'arms and legs' who can lift boxes and stack shelves. It's at this operational level that the whole 'recruit for attitude' ethos comes under significant pressure. This is where many fail. Consequently, store managers would normally blame inadequate staff for failing to achieve good customer engagement results, wrong for a number of reasons. And when asked how these inadequate employees ended up in their store, the answer would normally be along the lines of 'best of a bad bunch'.

From a service excellence perspective, once you start to lower your standards, you are storing up problems for the future and infecting your culture. When staff members start to see others not behaving in the organization's desired way, one of two things can happen. Either other staff begin to think that it's okay to behave in that way, or the offending individual is ejected as they don't fit. Neither outcome is a good one! This is a great example of short-term gain leading to long-term pain.

Much has already been written about the recruitment process at Pret, but to me this is the cornerstone of why their service is so good. As we've said, they are clear about what attributes they are looking for: it's a very early start, 5 am, and a very physically demanding job. They may pay well, but it takes a particular type of person to work there. As well as the behavioural interviews, they have the Pret Experience Day, where the candidate comes to work in the store for four hours and works in all areas of the store. This helps both the candidate and the business to decide whether this is the right fit for them. What is striking about this is that the candidate is assessed by a trained recruiter and the team they work with also provides feedback before the manager has the final sign-off. This creates a sort of unwritten contract between the candidate and the team that says, "We backed you, don't let us down." There is no pressure greater than peer pressure. Their recruitment process works and good customer service is evident during a busy lunchtime period for an organization with reasonably high attrition. That's incredible.

3) Onboarding and Induction

The most important time to set the standards of the organization for new employees is at the start of employment. For any values- and behaviour-based organizations, it is essential to set expectations in the induction period. This reinforcement is essential in the build-up of behaviours and establishing the right culture. For too many organizations, the induction is about running through health and safety protocols, confirming personal details, and getting a security pass.

The best organizations take induction very seriously. As we have already seen at Metro Bank, they go as far as calling it an 'immersion session'. Their colleagues really get to understand how they fit into the organization and what it's about – as well as do the conga! Apple has an induction session called "What Makes Apple Apple." Every person who works there has to attend to understand why they do what they do. This goes right down to why they design products the way they do, as well as the current strategy. Whenever you talk to an Apple colleague in a store, you always get the sense that they know what they are there to do and why. This mind-set is set up by an effective induction.

4) Training

I think I have made my views clear on 'sheep dip' customer-service training – hire the right people when it's really not necessary. However, most organizations already have tens, hundreds, and thousands of colleagues already serving customers. Shouldn't they all get customer-service training? Customer service training is to establish the standards that will be expected by the organization and perhaps help individuals understand the mechanics of communication, e.g. body language or dealing with conflict.

Where training is absolutely imperative to deliver service excellence is around the skills and knowledge to do the job. It's all well and good to have enthusiastic and friendly people, but if they don't have the right knowledge, then they are not really much help to the customers. Investing the appropriate time to ensure that colleagues have the right knowledge to do the job is another element that comes under pressure from operational demands. Often there is such a desire to get an individual onto the shop floor or into the contact centre that there is little time for sufficient training and learning to provide effective customer service, resulting in unhappy customers. Many of the best service organizations have realized this and have set up 'Centres of Excellence' for developing all their employees. Disney has the Disney Institute. Apple has Apple University, and McDonalds has McDonalds University. These institutions form the 'bedrock' of ensuring that employees have the right skills.

In many industries, skills and knowledge training is becoming even more important as digital channels are beginning to allow customers to answer simple queries and carry out simple transactions themselves. This particularly impacts contact centres, where most organizations are investing heavily in self-service in order to save on cost and improve the experience for customers. Essentially this means that customers are now dealing with simple transactions themselves and calling in about more complex enquires. These require a higher level of knowledge, and therefore the colleagues with more experience or better training. Consequently, this puts pressure on the 'recruit for attitude and not for skills' ethos, and managers of complex functions see it as more important to hire people with the right skills or intelligence so they can be trained quickly to effectively help customers.

There is no doubt that this is a difficult square to circle, and certainly, if you asked many customers, they may say that they just want to deal with someone who can deal with their query quickly and correctly, whether they are friendly or not. However, organizations that aspire to service excellence must look for both knowledge and friendliness. The answer is to improve the way that organizations train and support the knowledge and decision-making of their colleagues. There have been very few advances in the methods by which training is carried out, with the classroom environment still being the principle way that employees are trained.

Charles Jennings developed the concept of 70:20:10 learning, which states that employees only learn 10% of their knowledge in the classroom, 20% from their peers, and 70% 'on the job'. Bearing this in mind, organizations should invest in ways to supercharge the 90% of learning outside of the classroom by investing in technologies and cultural change that empowers this.

I have been involved in a system that enables different learning by making available bite-sized videos that individuals can access through various media, very similar to learning on YouTube, which is something most of us do every day. I believe that this is the future of learning in support of the 90% of learning that is outside the classroom. If organizations can truly crack this, then it will change the face of their recruitment policies and will allow them to really focus on attitudes rather than skills, even for the most complex roles.

5) Performance Reviews

Probably one of the most hotly debated subject areas in recent times has been the subject of performance reviews, something that exists in almost every organization. Most of the debate has been around how effective they are, and whether they honestly reflect the performance of an individual. In fact, some organizations are now considering doing away with the formal annual performance reviews. Performance reviews have become increasingly complex, especially with the advent of competency frameworks. They have almost become a technical exercise gifted on the organization by the people function, something that organizations really don't want. As a result, they often find the plethora of forms and increasingly complex scoring systems or the simplified ones too laborious to bother filling it in appropriately.

However, performance reviews are incredibly important, especially if the organization wants to focus on behaviours and output – the 'how' as well as the 'what'. Herein lies the real issue. If organizations want to recruit for attitude, then attitude and performance have to be a fundamental part of the performance assessment process. Most organizations understand this, and it appears to varying degrees in many performance review structures. However, the reality is that assessing behaviour is hard and many managers either don't know how to do it or don't feel comfortable doing it. Let's think of the five behaviours that we focused on at Sainsbury's; friendly, enthusiastic, helpful, genuine and knowledgeable. If you exclude 'knowledgeable', which you could argue is black and white, the others are pretty difficult to assess. The key to it is observation, being around, and watching how people perform. But in today's busy world, how practical is that?

Performance reviews are incredibly important to driving the right sorts of behaviours. Once you have decided on the required behaviours, it's fairly easy to write them into whatever competency framework you like. But that doesn't make it happen. The issues are creating the time to truly observe performance, understanding how to assess behavioural performance, and then how to be confident giving that feedback. The best organizations look to address these issues.

6) Advancement

Many organizations may call it talent management, but I think this may be a bit grand for what I have observed. In many of the service excellence organizations, it's easy to 'get on' – they promote significantly from within, and it is common to start in front-line service jobs and end up in leadership roles within a very quick time frame. This makes absolute sense, as most of these organizations have invested time in recruiting the right individuals in the first place, with the right behavioural mind-set as well as enthusiasm for the organization. Logic says that many of these people would be successful in the organization and therefore progress. The organization needs to aid that by ensuring that the right opportunities continually appear.

At Pret A Manger, it is possible to start as a team member and become a store manager within four years. This is partly due to their expansion and opportunities coming through that way, but also because they do not recruit externally to their first leadership position – the team leader. Essentially everyone in the organization performing the team leader role will have started as a team member and will remember what it was like to be a team member. This creates a huge number of lower-level leaders, recruited in the right way, with a passion for the business, and a working knowledge of the 'Pret way'. But, even though there is a leadership pathway and individuals have to attend a four-day course at the academy, it's interesting that people don't graduate by the course, but by their managers, when their managers feel they are ready to take on a leadership role. There are very similar advancement mechanisms in place at Metro Bank, McDonalds, and Apple. It's clear that the 'opportunity to get on' is a key driver in making colleagues engaged and committed to the business. In turn, colleagues demonstrate appropriate behaviours in order to advance, which is exactly what the organization requires, forming leaders all over the business, not only in typical leadership roles.

Getting This Right Creates Magic Moments

The people function is fundamental to driving service excellence in an organization. But managers and leaders play a pivotal role in making it all work too. It is key to focus on leaders and their capabilities to drive a customer-centric organization. It's also imperative to put the appropriate level of importance to recruiting the customer-facing staff. They are the brand of the organization, the last five yards to the customer are arguably the most important. Set the highest standards for the custodians of it!

People make the magic happen. If you ask anyone to give you an example of great service, it will almost always involve something incredible that an individual will have done, probably going out of the way to help, maybe bending or breaking a rule to make something right for the customer. We all will have our own favourite examples. Let's consider a few of my favourites.

- A McDonald's worker in Chicago became an online hero when a customer posted a story about an elderly disabled gentleman who had wheeled himself to the front of the queue and asked the cashier a question. The gentleman was difficult to understand, but he was saying, "Help me" and the cashier worked out that he needed help cutting up and eating his meal. Much to the surprise of everyone in the queue, the cashier shut down his till and disappeared to wash his hands and put gloves on. The cashier then sat down, cut up the meal, and helped customer eat it. Rather than being angry, the people in the queue were brought to tears.

- An elderly gentleman had completed his weekly shop at Sainsbury's; when presented with the total he realized that he didn't have his wallet. The customer was clearly upset, but instead of making him put the stuff back, the cashier found a way of saving the transaction to her till, which enabled her to pay for the shopping with her own money later. She told the customer that he could pay her back the next time he came into the store. The elderly gentleman was extremely grateful and left the store with his shopping. The very next day, the gentleman's daughter came to the store looking for the cashier, who happened to be off. She left the cashier a thank-you letter, a cheque for the amount of shopping, and a £20 note to say thank you. The colleague didn't want to accept this, and so donated it to a local charity. But a relationship had been established between that family and Sainsbury's for life.

- A few years ago, a young lady named Lucy Robinson wrote to the Sainsbury's customer services department, asking why Tiger Bread was called Tiger Bread (see *Figure 17* over the page).

Dear
Sainssssssssssssbbbbbbbbburys,

Why is tiger bread c\alled tiger bread?
It should be c\alled giraffe bread.

Love from Lily Robinson age $3^1/_2$

Figure 17: The Tiger Bread Letter

Lucy Robinson's note asking why Tiger Bread was called Tiger Bread.

One of the service agents, Chris King, responded that Lucy was right, thanked her for pointing it out, and offered her a voucher for some sweets – but all in the tone of voice that a young child would understand (see *Figure 18*).

Thank you for your letter. I think renaming tiger bread giraffe bread is a brilliant idea – it looks more like the blotches on a giraffe than the stripes on a tiger, doesn't it?

It is called tiger bread because the first baker who made it thought it looked stripey like a tiger. Maybe they were a bit silly.

I really liked reading your letter so I thought I'd send you a little present. I've put a £3 gift card in with this letter. If you ask your Mum or Dad to take you to Sainsbury's you could use it to buy some of your own Tiger Bread and maybe if mum and dad say it's OK you can get some sweeties too. Please tell an adult to wait 48 hours before using this card.

I'm glad you wrote in to us and hope you like spending your gift card. See you in store soon.

Your Sincerely,
Chris King (age 27 & 1/3)
Customer Manager

Figure 18: The Best Response Ever!

In return, Lucy received a handwritten note, a voucher for some sweets....
but best of all, the note reflected her age and interests.

He did this without asking and without instruction, but because he felt he should. This story went viral twice and created more publicity than the best public relations department could have arranged. And what's more, Tiger Bread is now called Giraffe Bread...well in Sainsburys at least!

As I said, we'll all have plenty of these examples. You can buy books full of them, some big and some small, but all memorable. When I experience or hear one of them, I find myself thinking, "How did this happen?" The answer will normally be that they're created by the selfless intuition of kind people who understand that they are there to do their best to help customers.

Where do these people come from and what makes them do what they do? It's just amazing personal qualities; you can't train people to be like that, they just are! They do things because they think that others would do the same for them. You need to find these people and create an environment for them to be themselves and make these things happen. And then you need to tell the stories of how their behaviours made customers feel. Stories are incredibly powerful in creating the culture of service excellence and massively underutilized by most organizations. They are essential in creating the right 'mood'.

Fear and Urban Myths

If good people exist, why don't we see even more outstanding customer-centric behaviour? One answer is fear. For both colleagues and leaders, there is a fear of doing something wrong and, more importantly, the consequences if they do. What I have always found interesting is I have worked with lots of organizations in which this fear is prevalent. However, at the same time, when we analyse the consequences of underperformance, there often isn't any; underperformance is often very poorly managed. If that is the case, why aren't people taking more risks, knowing that if they get it wrong, there are hardly any implications?

This is often due to what I call 'the curse of the urban myth'. Stories are incredibly powerful, both positive and negative ones. All that is required is one about a manager who tried to do something, got it badly wrong, and was taken to the nearest coffee shop and fired (it's always a coffee shop!). It can cause a whole organization to follow the rules and stop pushing the boundaries. Often that means not doing the right thing for customers, even when the right thing is plainly obvious. Negative stories like this are rarely true, or difficult to trace anyone who knows for sure that it happened, which is why I call them urban myths. I think they are often a convenient reason for people to be cautious and take the easy option of following a rule or making a decision that is clearly not in the best interest of the customer. Remember what happened to the last guy who crossed the line?

The number of times I have had to deal with serious complaints, when I have despaired that good people hadn't made the right decisions, even though it was plainly obvious, when you ask staff "Why?" The answer is always fear. So we come back again to environment. Great leaders create an environment where good people feel safe to make decisions, knowing that it might be wrong and prepared to grow as a result of it. As in a cult, if the belief is that 'we're all in it together' and **it's okay to be 'wrong for the right reason'**, then there is every opportunity that magic can happen on a sustainable basis. Creating this sort of environment is difficult, but is key to developing the empowerment that most organizations crave.

As well as having the right leaders and finding the right people, the organization also has to think a bit differently, too. A great example is QVC, where ensuring that the frontline colleagues feel empowered is imperative. At QVC they encourage colleagues to solve customer problems without ever having to refer anything to a manager. If an agent has to refer something to a manager, then they receive coaching. This is not as a form of punishment, but to ensure that if the same situation were to occur again, the agent would be able to effectively resolve it without feeling the need to refer the problem to a manager. The QVC working environment is geared to colleagues finding a way to solve problems themselves. This is a great example of pushing decision making down to the front line, where it really matters.

Every organization wants their colleagues to be more empowered; it's like the 'Holy Grail' of business. I remember talking to Craig Kreeger, the CEO of Virgin Atlantic, about how he was returning the airline to profit. He said the hardest thing to do was to convince the cabin crews that it was okay for them to make decisions 'in the moment' to do whatever they needed to do to make the customers happy.

Changing the environment is hard and takes time, and sticking to it is key. Even great people will not feel empowered where there is fear. For there to be no fear, there needs to be trust (see *Figure 19*).

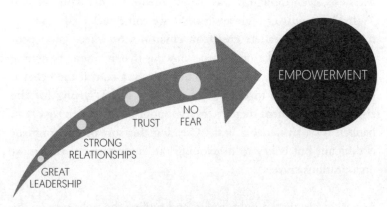

Figure 19: The Empowerment Curve
Great leadership comes from strong relationships, trust, respect and no fear.

For there to be trust there has to be strong relationships, and for there to be strong relationships, there needs to be great leadership. At Virgin Atlantic, Craig has created a vision: **"To embrace the human spirit and let it fly."** I can't think of anything more apt.

CHAPTER NINE

Stop Doing Dumb Stuff to Customers

I once had a conversation with Justin King, CEO of Sainsbury's, about the number of complaints received from customers about colleagues being 'rude'. The numbers of such complaints was insignificant compared to the volume of transactions that we did on a weekly basis. However, it was always a concern. No one in the organization, outside of the complaints team, read and responded to more customer complaints than Justin, so he had an almost unique understanding of how customers felt. It's actually a key determinant to how customer-focused an organization is – how involved the CEO gets with customer issues. Justin was determined to ensure all issues were appropriately resolved, which didn't mean the customer was always right, but it did mean everyone in the organization being brutally honest about how the organization had performed.

How Dumb Stuff Happens ...

Justin believed that these complaints fell into three categories:

- The colleague was probably rude
- The customers didn't like the answer they were given
- Policy created by the organization put the colleague in a difficult situation and clearly created the wrong answer for the customer.

In the final category, if the colleague doesn't feel empowered to overturn a policy, then the organization ends up doing 'dumb stuff' for customers. All organizations need processes and rules, and these are normally created to cover the majority of situations – even if they are created on the 80/20 rule, which leaves 20% of instances where they don't work. There has never been a more important time for organizations to understand their processes from customers' perspectives, truly understanding the journey of the processes that they send customers on, from start to finish.

At Sainsbury's, I once received a complaint letter that I later I used as a 'bell weather' for customer-centric decision making. The letter was from a 73-year-old retired gentleman who had been going to a particular Sainsbury's café for the previous seven years for breakfast with his wife before doing their weekly shop. The gentleman didn't like bacon in his breakfast and would ask to swap it for a sausage, and he'd done so for seven years. One day, when he asked for his customary 'swap', he was told about a new directive from the head office that he couldn't swap. If he wanted the extra sausage, he would have to pay extra.

He challenged this to no avail, even when he spoke to the manager. So he wrote in to the head office to say that he wasn't going to set foot in the store again. Internally, everyone agreed that it was a bad outcome, but not everyone agreed that it was a bad decision by the store. Many people said that they should have just swapped the sausage, while others believed that they were right to follow the rule and such a clearly un-customer friendly rule should not have been issued and that was the problem. The lesson here is that everyone in an organization should be thinking of the impact that decisions have on a customer. Colleagues should feel empowered to overrule something that they believe to be wrong or unnecessary.

In this particular case, the lifetime value of a customer is another important point that must be considered. Swapping the bacon for the sausage was an additional 80p , which is not much when considering all the money the customer had ever spent in a Sainsbury's and the future revenue that it would lose. Put in that context, we would switch the sausage every time! Decision making can be difficult at the best of times, but if we could encourage colleagues to see the big picture and the lifetime value of a customer, I think many situations would work out differently.

Most organizations have a thorough understanding of their processes from an 'inside-out' perspective. They can often produce numerous process maps to show how things work and indicate what the interactions are with customers and how long different steps should take. The use of process maps was considered okay and still is in many quarters. However, these process maps and service level agreements have little to do with how it feels for the customers, so now the key is to understand the processes and rules from an outside-in perspective. How does this feel for the customers and how can we make it better for them. The emotional element is key; how the process makes customers feel is often what they will remember. It's impossible to create a service excellence environment without understanding how your processes impact customers, especially since now with the increase in the number of transactions in the digital world, fewer and fewer processes involve a human.

Delivering consistently good experiences for customers is important. By having the right individual in the right moment, organizations can create 'wow' experiences, but I'm a great believer in delivering consistently good experiences that allow magic to flourish. Getting it right day in and day out, week in and week out, is normally enough for most people to be 'wowed'. The reality is that ***consistently good service doesn't happen by accident***; it only happens by design. There are three elements to this though. First, understanding the existing customer journey completely; second, being brave enough to reengineer your processes to improve the customer journey; and lastly, being committed to operational standards that can deliver the desired experience. It's only when all three of these are in place that this can really work, so let's consider them in turn.

Understanding the Customer Journey

This really is a case of 'walking in the customers shoes', trying to understand not only what they experience, but also what they think before, during, and after the experience. A customer's journey can be represented in five phases; collectively I like to refer to these as the E5 model:

- **Evaluation** – this is when customers are thinking about interacting with an organization or a variety of others. They might be thinking about going shopping at a store or online. For example, on a shopping trip a customer might think about making a shopping list. And where will they be able to park when they get there? And so on. It is important to understand these thought processes in order to predict if the existing processes impact what the customer is thinking and if there is anything that could be done to improve the experience. As a differentiator, this evaluation stage of the customer experience may be the difference between securing business and losing it. In the online world, Google has called this the 'zero moment of truth'. How easy you make it to find your website or make it come up in a search is vital.

- **Entry** – this includes all the things that happen at the start of the process, incredibly important because first impressions die hard. These first experiences set up the whole journey, and in some cases define whether the journey will take place at all. I have seen many a shopping trip abandoned at the front door.

- **Experience** – this is the substantive process. How does it work for the customer? What are the key touch points and the 'moments of truth' that really matter to a customer?

- **Exit** – how is the process completed or ended? Is it in a way that provides a great feeling for customers and gives them all the information that they need or require? In a retail environment, it's all about queuing and checking out and the interactions around that.

- **Extension** – this is what happens after the process that helps build the relationship with the customers. For example, if they have bought something, a call to enquire whether everything is working okay, or maybe some vouchers for a return trip, or even a post-experience questionnaire. Anything that cements the experience.

The key to this is learning and understanding how customers feel after every interaction with the organization. The only way to do that is to ask. Many organizations do this now through 'touch-point feedback surveys' where they ask customers how they feel at key touch points or 'moments of truth'. Even small organizations that may not have access to enterprise-wide feedback systems, it's just as valid to simply ask customers and be aware of the reasons why customers are complaining, which tells the organization a lot about dissatisfied customers.

Reengineering the Processes

When mapping the existing journey for customers, the key is to understand the 'pain points' and the key customer touch points or 'Moments of Truth'. These are the points that disproportionately drive how customers feel about their experiences. At this point, it becomes like the 'continuous improvement' loop and the organization must decide how committed it is to reengineering a particular process or even innovating a completely new way. This can be very challenging because something that makes things easier for the customer could make it significantly more difficult and more costly for the organization. It depends on the organization's appetite to change for the customers and, quite simply, the costs of doing it, compared to the benefits. The issue becomes how to commercially assess the long term impact of making something easier for customers, which is why such projects are often a leap of faith.

Apple is a master of this and has reinvented the shopping experience for customers by focusing on things that provide marginal gains for customers, but create a legendary reputation. One of these is the way that they bring the checkout to the customer, the assistants' PDA devices allow the customer to pay where they are standing and the product is brought to them. The system for doing that is complex and it is likely expensive, but it enabled Apple to do something that no other company could do at that time. Even if lots of organizations copy this service, in time Apple will always be the first to have done it – customer experience has a real 'first mover' advantage!

For an innovative company focused on he customer experience, Apple has a fascinating attitude to prioritisation, as this quote from Tim Cook, the current CEO, outlines:

> "We are the most focused company that I know of or have read of or have any knowledge of. **We say no to good ideas every day. We say no to great ideas** in order to keep the amount of things we focus on very small in number so that we can put enormous energy behind the ones we do choose."

This addresses one of the many reasons that organizations struggle to improve their customers' experiences, even though they have been through extensive customer journey mapping initiatives. They simply try to do too much. Journey mapping will always throw up a plethora of things to do; the key is to prioritize a few that will make a real difference to customers and can be executed with ruthless focus, measuring progress along the way (see *Figure 20*).

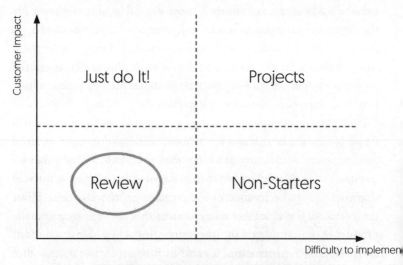

Figure 20: Customer Improvement Prioritisation Matrix
Organizations trying to become more customer-centric
can face a range of obstacles.

Once the 'what' that needs changing has been established, the 'how' comes sharply into focus. *Great service is created by those who deliver it*: employees and colleagues. Gathering a team of great colleagues from different parts of the business and giving them a customer issue to resolve garners great results and improves collaboration among the groups that need to make it happen.

Just as important as involving colleagues in evolving new processes is involving customers. Customers are the only ones able to tell you whether a new process has met it objectives, but probably more importantly how it can be improved further. This works particularly well when the improvement is for a specific target group that will help to find solutions that would work for them. Co-creation works very well for improving the customer journey.

Within the whole ideation and innovation process, it's really important that there are no sacred cows. There are things that may have been successful for some time and produced good results; they may even be what the organization is known for, but times change, as does the business environment and customer preferences. So it's important to continually test widely held beliefs in case they no longer hold true. This was perfectly illustrated when I was talking to Tracy Garrard of First Direct. They are famous for the fact that when you ring them you get straight through to a human voice and that they do not use Interactive Voice Response (IVR) systems. This is their 'special sauce'. However, in looking at how they can improve things for customers, even they have had to consider whether a policy that has been in place since they came into existence almost 30 years ago still has relevance in the current digital world. Tracy was clear that this couldn't be a sacred cow and has to be continually evaluated and considered on its merits compared to other solutions and possible improvements. It's still in place, but the special sauce doesn't necessarily stay special forever.

Innovation is nothing without high operational standards of execution

To create a service excellence culture, everyone in the organization has to understand and buy into the high performance standards at all points. This is not just a matter for the customer-facing staff; it applies equally to internal services as well. *If you're not serving a customer, you're probably serving someone who is!* Aside from the metrics and governance in place to measure customers' expectations, service standards should be frequently reviewed throughout the organization with a low tolerance for errors or non-performance. The problem with most SLAs is that they are usually aggregated and allow a reasonable amount of wiggle room for poor or average performance to sneak in. This may appear to customers like inconsistent service, and therefore it's imperative to set challenging on-going targets, knowing that things will sometimes go wrong. However, there should be some processes or moments of truth that have zero tolerance and have a 100% success rate.

At Sainsbury's online shopping business, complaints received began to increase, even though there was no change to the percentage of on time deliveries, which was on target. When we looked into it, we discovered that the issue was not late deliveries themselves, but we had a policy that if a driver was going to be late, then he should call the customer. We measured this and the percentage of calls made had actually dropped and in actual fact the key metric in this process was not just the percentage of late deliveries, but the percentage of late deliveries where the call was made. We set the target for calls made on late deliveries at 100%, zero tolerance, and guess what, – the complaints dried up.

Without great operational execution, any redesign of the customer experience is pointless. A good example of this is when Starbucks redesigned the order process so that as well as asking for you coffee order, the baristas' would also ask for your name. This would ideally create a closer connection with their customers, so that you were no longer a faceless 'grande latte with a shot', then you were John or Jane! This is a great idea but the issue is, since the introduction of this policy the baristas' still often shout, "S 'skinny cappuccino'!"

What's the point of asking customers to give their names, if you aren't going to execute the process properly? It's all about high standards, leadership, and maybe explaining to all the colleagues the 'why' as well as the 'what'!

Essentially organisation must understand the customer journey, identify and design the key moments of truth, create appropriate measures, set high standards, and establish appropriate governance to ensure that it all happens simply. If only!

There is no doubt that designing and executing a superior customer experience can be a key differentiator for organizations and we have plenty of examples from some of the best: Apple, Amazon, Disney, John Lewis, Virgin Atlantic, and First Direct. One organization that is creating a completely different proposition to its competitors is Metro Bank. As well as getting their culture right, their experience is completely differential. Whether it's allowing customers to bring in dogs, the free Magic Money machines or free pens ... these things define who they are; they're not gimmicks. However, what proves to me that they are thinking about customers when designing their processes and operating policies is their opening hours. Most banks operate when their customers are at work; they open at 10 am and shut at 4 pm, and are closed on weekends, which is crazy. But Metro Bank is open 362 days of the year, from 8am – 8pm on Monday to Friday and most of the day on Saturdays and Sundays. This shows its customers that Metro Bank is there for them when it suits the customers. Maybe this is one of the reasons why Metro Bank is the fastest-growing bank in the western world ... not bad for a customer cult! Follow your customers and they will reward you for it!

CHAPTER TEN

Turning the Flywheel

A flywheel is a heavy rotational wheel that is hard to turn, but once it gets going it creates its own momentum and is used to create energy.

We started with a definition, so I thought we should end with one. I have always described establishing a service excellence culture in an organization as a bit like a flywheel: very difficult to get going, but once it is established, it has its own momentum and requires infrequent interventions to keep it going.

Customer experience programmes can also be described as being on a fad diet. Everyone wants to lose weight, but they want to do it the easy way, so they make quick progress that is encouraging initially, but they soon grow tired of it, stop doing the right things, and quickly put the weight back on. The reality is that there's no easy way to achieve service excellence. It's about belief, hard work, difficult decisions, discipline and sustainability – a bit like a diet.

We've been through the main components that are required to build service excellence:

- Have a clear purpose, vision, and commitment to doing the best for your customers.
- Understand your customers' needs and expectations, monitor these, and continually try to improve on them.
- Establish a service leadership group throughout the business to create the right environment where service culture can grow and thrive.
- Recruit people with the right capabilities to provide service excellence to your customers, external or internal. Carefully observe performance and manage the behaviours of existing employees.
- Understand your existing processes from a customer perspective and set extremely high operational standards.
- Establish effective governance for all of the above.

As I continually say, it looks simple, but it's not easy for many, many reasons!

And that brings me to two last questions that people ask me. First, do you need to do the service excellence initiatives in any particular order? I don't think so. In fact, all elements don't have to be in place for progress to be made. Lots of organizations make a big deal about implementing customer feedback and NPS programmes, and see an improvement as a result of that, because if you shine a light on anything, you will probably see improvement. However, it won't be sustainable without the other elements. It makes sense to establish a vision and purpose and commitment to customers first; otherwise, there is nothing to guide the decision making when the going gets tough. This is pretty much always where I would start.

It's also important to note how long it would take the various elements of the model to have an impact. Establishing good customer metrics and reviewing processes can create quick short-term benefits, while they bed in over the longer term. All the elements that relate to people and leadership not only take longer to implement, but also take longer to have an impact, especially dependent on what the position of the organization is at the start of the change and the commitment the organization puts into implementation.

Next, it is important to maintain momentum – keeping the flywheel turning! More specifically, consider if in order to make a specific thing happen, should it be somebody's full-time job in the organization? This as a consideration depends on the maturity of the organization in relation to customer centricity.

Within the top customer-centric organizations highlighted throughout this book, all employees know that they exist in order to benefit the customer and it's part of everybody's job. It's so embedded in the business that it just happens. It will rarely be the case that establishing and executing an end-to-end service excellence strategy will be the sole responsibility for a particular individual alone. The absence of somebody with sole responsibility doesn't necessarily mean that you are looking at a customer-centred business. In fact, organizations at the other end of the spectrum that are not focused on customers at all often do not have someone focused on service excellence either.

This leaves all the organizations that are somewhere on the journey to achieving service excellence, which is in reality, most organizations. For those, I think it helps to have someone who is championing not only the customer and managing the various initiatives to improve things for the customer, but is also there to question decisions that the organization might make that could be considered not customer centric and hold leaders' feet to the flames.

All change is like an elastic band. Enthusiasm, good ideas, and initiatives can stretch it, but there's always a pull to bring back the status quo, the way that things used to be and with that pull, ideas and initiatives can wither and die. Keeping the elastic stretched and the flywheel turning requires not only enthusiasm, but evangelism. It requires leaders clear on their intent and a group of loyal followers to make it all happen. Sounds a bit like a cult to me!

...but surely being a cult is a bad thing?

We've covered a lot of ground, but ultimately what I'm proposing is that, in order to create a high performing service excellence culture in an organisation which consistently delivers for its customers and engenders a feeling of Love, that organisation has to behave a bit like a cult…and cults are bad, right? There's no doubt that there are bad cults out there, but they're not all bad. At their core there is a central belief or ideology that everyone in the cult believes in. Everything flows from that ideology, whether it's the leadership style, the behaviour of the followership, how people are recruited or the perception of the cult to the outside world. Belief in the ideology is at its core. Such devout commitment to the ideology may make a cult difficult to understand for people who are not part of it, the sense that they are 'different'. But, as I said, different doesn't always mean bad.

I believe that in order to provide exceptional service experience to their customers on a consistent basis, organisations must have customer experience as their central ideology, above and beyond all else. This is incredibly difficult to do for most organisations, not because they don't value customers, but because they struggle to trade off doing the right things for customers against the normal commercial pressures of running a business. That's why having a cult-like belief in meeting customer needs is so important, it helps clarify decision making for everyone throughout the organisation.

The concept of being more customer centric is not new. However, it is brought into sharper focus by the shift in the balance of power between customers and organisations. Enabled by technology, particularly mobile, customers are able to have a voice like never before, this voice can make or break even the largest organisations. A company's brand is no longer what their marketing and PR department says about them, it's what their customers say. This new level of transparency means that establishing a seamless and consistent customer experience has never been so important, failure to do so can hugely undermine a business. Customer experience is also now a huge source of sustainable competitive advantage, and is being used by the most committed organizations to differentiate them from the rest of their market. Service innovation and differentiation is becoming as important as product was previously and as markets become more and more commoditised, the focus on service experience will continue to grow.

If you want to create a cult around service excellence in an organisation, it's simple, it's just not easy! The Service Excellence model (*Figure 6*) provides the pointers to success.

A cult is all about everybody in the organization believing in the overall purpose. In the case of service excellence, it's about everybody believing that the reason that the organization exists is for it to do the right things for customers and, that in doing so, all the other things about being a successful organization will take care of themselves. For example, the products will be right, the services consistently good, and the brand will remain strong and highly recognisable.

To be a service excellence cult organization requires a clear vision and purpose that everyone can believe in, and this is normally created by a visionary leader who is unflinching in their commitment to the service excellence ideology. They enure that there is a vision, mission and values that reflect this commitment to customers and they work really hard to ensure that it is embedded into the business. Everyone in the business needs to be able to 'Hum the Tune'. This is not a one-off activity, it is a constant as the organisation continues to evolve and people leave and join.

In order to ensure that this vision and its associated values are embedded in the organization, strong leadership is required throughout the organization that drives the belief in customers and has zero tolerance for divergence from understanding customer needs, consistently delivering to them, and continually innovating to improve things for customers. These service leaders are obsessive about creating the right environment where all their colleagues can thrive in pursuit of the same goals. They do this by ensuring that they are:

- Visible, available and build relationships with their teams which create both trust and respect.
- Inspiring the team by ensuring that they understand how they fit in with objectives of the organization and communicate progress with passion.
- Accountable for the actions and results of the team, whilst also promoting ownership within the team, They create a safe environment for their team to take risks and grow as a result.

- Clear on the needs of their particular customers, understand how they are performing and work with their team on how to improve things.

The most significant outcomes from great Service Leadership are trust and respect. If leaders have this they can achieve almost anything.

Every cult needs its followers. The employees need to not only believe in the vision and values, but they must have a clear understanding of what behaviour is required of them in order to thrive in the organization and why these beliefs and behaviours will make the organization serve its customers better. The organisation needs to ensure that these employee behaviours are embedded into every element of the employee lifecycle, especially recruitment, on-boarding and performance reviews. There needs to be cult-like 'organ rejection' of employees that do not 'fit' and exhibit the right behaviours. The organization, as a result, is full of people with the same value set, so it is engaging and empowering to work in.

Doing the right thing for customers and ensuring that they are happy needs to be an obsession. Therefore, the organisations need to be clear on the needs of their customer, ensuring that they understand the 'Fundamental Truths' of what their customer needs. They must then ensure they have a balanced suite of metrics that ensure that they understand how they are doing for customers, and more importantly helps them understand what they need to do to improve…it's the virtuous cycle of customer improvement. For this to work they need to have the correct governance in place to ensure that the customer intelligence is being understood and that improvements are being appropriately prioritized and actioned. Employees should be recognised and rewarded for achieving the right customer outcomes.

Lastly, the organisation must understand their processes and procedures from their customer's perspective. They need to understand any 'pain points' and innovate to improve these. They should also understand the 'moments of truth' and work tirelessly to deliver in these moments. Operational excellence is essential and everyone in the organisation must be focused on delivering to the highest standards, consistently. Being brilliant at the basics, is absolutely fundamental. However, if the process isn't right or produces the wrong outcome for customers, then the colleagues need to be empowered to change them.

So it's clear that becoming a service excellence cult is not easy, there are lots of things to achieve and plenty of external pressures that will work against it being achieved. Additionally, working in this type of culture can be tough, the continual focus on improving things for customers and the obsession with delivering the highest standards can be wearing on even the most dedicated of employees. However, the world is changing fast and customers hold the 'whip hand'. With technology driving ever increasing transparency, customers will no longer accept poor service and will punish those who provide it. Conversely, they will reward those organisations who can consistently meet their ever evolving needs, and these organisations will end up as the 'winners' in the end. In order to achieve this, organizations will need to be a bit more like cults.

An Introduction to
Oke Eleazu

Oke Eleazu, Managing Director of the consulting business, think outside in, which helps organizations take a strategic approach to improving their customer experience and operational performance by focusing on having the right culture and leadership in place. He has had a number of blue chip clients. Oke has held several senior roles in major organizations, all centered on improving the experience of customers. Most recently he has been Director of Customer Service Strategy for Sainsbury's, where he created and executed a new strategy for delivering ever improving service for Sainsbury's 24 million customers a week through 160,000 colleagues. Sainsbury's won the Grocer Gold Award for Customer Service in 2013, 2014 and 2015 and were nominated for Customer Strategy of the Year at the prestigious UK Customer Experience Awards in 2014. He is also an in demand International conference speaker, having recently spoken in Barcelona, Amsterdam, Johannesburg and Dubai, as well as all over the UK. He is also the chair of the prestigious International Customer Experience Conference in Rome.

Oke is also currently a non-executive director of the Institute of Customer Service and Bromford Housing Group where he is vice Chair and chairs the Customer and Communities Board.

Previously he was Customer Service and Operations Director for Bupa, where he delivered a number of initiatives for people, process and technology to maintain Bupa's reputation for first class service. Previously, Oke was Customer Delivery Director at Prudential. Oke had Approved Person responsibilities at both Bupa and the Prudential and led the TCF initiatives at both organizations. In 2005, he led the Pru to win the prestigious Management Today/Unisys Service Excellence Award for Financial Services.

CONCISE ADVICE LAB

SMALL BOOKS: BIG IDEAS

CLEVER CONTENT, DYNAMIC
IDEAS, PRACTICAL SOLUTIONS
AND ENGAGING VISUALS –
A CATALYST TO INSPIRE NEW
WAYS OF THINKING AND
PROBLEM-SOLVING IN A
COMPLEX WORLD

The Mindfulness Book • The Brain Book • The Meeting Book • The Attitude Book
The Diagrams Book • The Impact Code • The Productivity Habits • The Ideas Book
The Networking Book • The Success Book • The Feedback Book • The Smart Thinking Book
The Future Book • The Storytelling Book • The Financial Wellbeing Book
The Visual Communications Book • The Business Bullshit Book

£9.99 / $15.95
conciseadvicelab.com